THE BEST OF
BIRDS & BLOOMS
2011

Contents

40

123

85

Letter From the Editor, 4

CHAPTER 1 / Amazing Birds, 6

CHAPTER 2 / Budget Backyards, 42

CHAPTER 3 / Photo How-To, 68

CHAPTER 4 / Magnificent Hummingbirds, 88

CHAPTER 5 / Beautiful Blooms, 118

CHAPTER 6 / Great Escapes, 152

CHAPTER 7 / Butterflies Galore, 178

CHAPTER 8 / DIY Backyard, 200

BONUS CHAPTER 9 / Growing Veggies, 222

Index, 248

EASTERN BLUEBIRD, RICHARD DAY / DAYBREAK IMAGERY

We're back! We're excited to once again present the *Best of Birds & Blooms*. In this 2011 edition, you'll find great birding and gardening tips, along with stories and advice from the past year. And best of all, it's in one convenient spot! Looking for our popular "All-American Birds" article from this summer? It's in here! Or what about the stories from our special hummingbird and budget issues? Those are included, too! Here at *Birds & Blooms*, we're birders and gardeners ourselves, so we're right alongside you, trying out reader tips and looking for answers from our talented experts. Thanks for your support over the years and giving us a reason to develop this "Best of" series. We can't wait to see what's around the corner.

Stacy Tornio
Editor, *Birds & Blooms*

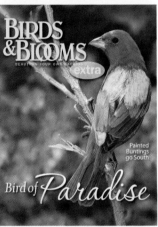

Birds & Blooms

Stacy Tornio Editor
Sue Myers Art Director
Crystal Rennicke Senior Editor
Becky Denham Wernlund Project Art Director
Trudi Bellin Photo Coordinator
Joanne Weintraub, Dulcie Shoener Copy Editors
Dena Ahlers Production Coordinator
Mary Ann Koebernik Assistant Photo Coordinator
Danielle Calkins Assistant Editor/Digital
Lorie West Editorial Assistant
George Harrison, Melinda Myers, Tom Allen
Contributing Editors

Heather Lamb Executive Editor
Sharon K. Nelson Creative Director
Deb Warlaumont Mulvey Copy Chief

Catherine Cassidy Vice President, Editor in Chief
Heidi Reuter Lloyd Vice President, Executive Editor/Books
Mark Hagen Senior Editor/Books

Lisa Karpinski North American Chief Marketing Officer
Dan Fink Vice President/Book Marketing

The Reader's Digest Association, Inc.

Mary G. Berner President and
Chief Executive Officer
Suzanne M. Grimes President, North American Affinities

© 2010 Reiman Media Group, LLC
5400 S. 60th St., Greendale WI 53129-1404

International Standard Book Number:
0-89821-871-3
978-0-89821-871-8

Serial Number: 1553-8400

On the Cover:
Blue grosbeak, Richard Day / Daybreak Imagery;
Arctic primrose, Darryl R. Beers

For additional copies of this book
or information on other books, write:
Birds & Blooms Customer Service, P.O. Box 5294,
Harlan IA 51593-0794;
call toll-free: 800-344-6913;
e-mail: *rpsubscustomercare@custhelp.com*.
Visit our website at *birdsandblooms.com*

Amazing Birds

From urban birding and all-American favorites to nesting marvels and reader bird tales, we have a little bit of everything in this year's roundup.

Welcome Back Orioles **8**

Nesting Marvels **12**

Winter Wonderland **16**

Berries for Birds **19**

Birding in the Big City **20**

All-American Birds **24**

Bird Tales **30**

The Secret Lives of Owls **34**

Backyard Birding Solutions **38**

Photos of the Year **40**

LINDA ARNDT

The early bird gets the worm when it comes to attracting these beauties.

By Anne Schmauss

Baltimore oriole

welcome back orioles

Last April, I was picking up clothes from my daughter's bedroom floor when my eye caught a flash of orange outside her window. Dirty socks in hand, I was stopped in my tracks by the sight of a brilliant orange and black Bullock's oriole. There he was, clinging to my flower basket, plucking and eating the red blossoms from my geraniums. *Oh no,* I thought, *I don't have my feeder out!*

It was mid-April in New Mexico, and I knew orioles were already arriv-

8

Chapter 1

Bullock's oriole

FRIEND OR FOE?

Orioles often get a bad rap. Many farmers don't like these fliers because they go after fruit crops. But for most birders, the orioles' brilliant plumage is a welcome addition to a backyard, and bird lovers will do anything possible to attract these bright songbirds.

ing. Customers at my bird store had reported seeing them for a week or so, but procrastination got the best of me. Normally a bit of laziness doesn't make much difference when feeding birds, but with orioles, timing is everything!

After a few minutes, my oriole flew off. Moving quickly, I found my oriole feeder, filled it with sugar water and hung it outside. I never saw the orange guy come back, though.

For the next couple of weeks, I faithfully filled the feeder with fresh nectar

every few days, but it was too late.

Orioles are stunning birds, much anticipated by bird lovers. Even though males are brighter, females are gorgeous fliers as well.

You can find nine orioles in the United States, but only five are common.

Baltimore and orchard orioles are widespread in the East, and the Bullock's is found throughout the West. The Scott's and hooded orioles are common in the Southwest, but you can see the four other orioles only at

the extreme southern edge of Texas or Florida.

Orioles spend their winters in Mexico and Central and South America, where they can find a steady source of insects, fruit and nectar. Then they migrate north to nest in early spring.

And what a nest it is! Many orioles look for tall deciduous trees, where they carefully weave together plant fiber and sometimes yarn or string.

Some orioles will take up to 12 days to construct their pendulous

A bit of laziness doesn't make much difference when feeding birds, but with orioles, timing is everything.

sac-shaped nests on the ends of slender branches. This precarious placement keeps the eggs and babies relatively safe from climbing predators and other nest robbers.

Your chance to see orioles doesn't last long, because most start to migrate south in August. It's a thrill to see these beautiful and sometimes elusive songbirds. Whether you spot them for just a day or are lucky enough to have them visit your yard most of the summer, they are one of spring's greatest bird treasures.

Anne Schmauss is the co-author of For the Birds: A Month-by-Month Guide to Attracting Birds to Your Backyard.

Bullock's oriole

all in the family

Baltimore oriole. This stunning black-and-orange bird is found throughout the Midwestern and Eastern U.S. It is very similar in appearance to its Western cousin, the Bullock's oriole. In fact, at one time both species were considered the same and were called the northern oriole. Their ranges overlap in the middle of the country. Some Baltimore orioles spend their winters as far north as the extreme Southeast coast of the U.S.

Bullock's oriole. Bullock's orioles are the most widespread orioles in the West, where they prefer to nest in tall trees along streams and rivers. They are named in honor of William Bullock and his son, who did extensive ornithological work in Mexico in the early 1800s. Bullock's orioles love grasshoppers and will feast on them almost exclusively when they are plentiful.

Orchard oriole. The orchard oriole is the smallest oriole in North America and is common throughout the Midwest and East, though you may not see it as often as the Baltimore because it rarely visits nectar feeders. The orchard oriole comes a bit later than other orioles in the spring and sometimes heads south as early as mid-July.

Scott's oriole. Commonly seen in the arid Southwest, the Scott's is hard to miss. The male is lemon-yellow and black and readily comes to nectar feeders. Although many orioles nest in very tall trees, the Scott's often nests in the relatively short yucca plant. It also eats nectar from the yucca flowers and uses fibers taken from dead yucca for nest building.

Hooded oriole. The hooded oriole is also found in the Southwest and is named for the male's orange hood. This small, slender oriole often builds her nest in palm trees, where she literally sews the saclike nest onto a palm leaf.

attracting orioles

Start early. Your best chance of attracting orioles is when they first arrive in early spring.

Use the **same nectar recipe for orioles as you do for hummingbirds**—four parts boiled water to one part sugar. Keep nectar fresh, and don't use food coloring.

These birds are **attracted to the color orange**, so look for a sugar-water feeder specifically designed for orioles.

Make sure your **feeder has large enough perches and drinking ports**. It's not unusual for orioles to try hummingbird feeders, but their bills are often too big.

Orioles love the color and taste of oranges. Offer orange halves on a branch or feeder.

Orioles will also eat grape jelly. Serve the jelly in an open dish or cup, and keep it fresh.

When placing the oriole feeder in your yard, **think like a bird**. Instead of hiding the feeder under an awning or tree, **put it out in the open so the birds can see it while flying overhead.**

Hang your feeder near a birdbath. If your bath has a bubbler, even better. Orioles love the sight and sound of moving water.

Put out yarn and string. Orioles and other backyard songbirds will use it for their nests.

If you don't attract orioles in your first year, keep at it. **It often takes several seasons to find a following.**

A BITE TO EAT. This female Bullock's oriole gives a fledgling a little snack.

Orchard oriole

Scott's oriole

Hooded oriole

nesting marvels

Discover some of the most amazing nesters in North America.

By George Harrison, Contributing Editor

When most people think of a bird's nest, they probably imagine a grassy little bowl, held together with weed stalks and mud, in the crook of a tree. While this does describe the typical nest of an American robin, it doesn't even come close for many other backyard birds.

Though nests all serve the same purpose—to secure the eggs and young—the shape, depth, material and location vary greatly. Sizes range anywhere from a hummingbird's golf-ball-size nest covered in lichens to a bald eagle's giant platform of sticks, high in a treetop and sometimes weighing more than a ton.

Nearly every species has its own unique nesting habits. Take a look at some of the most fascinating nesters in the birding world.

Burrowing owl. Like foxes and woodchucks, some birds nest underground. But the burrowing owl just might be the most unusual. Most other owls nest in cavities, shelters or on the ground, but this flier actually digs its own 4- to 8-foot tunnel. It lays its eggs on the far end of the chamber. When the owlets are old enough to be curious, you can see their heads poking up at the entrance of a nesting burrow, looking around like kit foxes.

Belted kingfisher. Also an underground nester, the belted kingfisher digs its own burrow in the bare earth near the top of an exposed bank along a lake or river.

THE GOLDEN YEARS

Long-lived birds such as hawks, owls, geese and swans will continue mating and laying eggs as long as they live. In England, a captive pair of eagle owls regularly mated and produced eggs for 32 years, raising no fewer than 93 young!

Chimney swift. Many birds make their own glue to hold their nests together. In China, a swift makes its entire nest from a gluelike substance it excretes from its bill. Here in North America, the chimney swift uses its gluey saliva to stick its nest to the inside of chimneys. Another common bird that glues its nest with mud is the barn swallow.

Common murre. Among the seabirds, the common murre will lay its eggs on the bare ledge of a sea cliff. The shape of the eggs offers natural protection: They're long ovals with pointed ends, which makes them roll in a circle and not over the cliff.

American coot. A handful of waterbirds will build floating nests, creating small islands. The American coot typically constructs a cupped platform of cattails, rotted bulrushes or reeds, floating on 1 to 4 feet of water and attached to nearby aquatic plants.

Two American robin eggs and two brown-headed cowbird eggs in the same nest

STAN OSOLINSKI / DEMBINSKY PHOTO ASSOCIATES

Great horned owl. Like the peregrine falcon, the California condor and other raptors, this owl may construct a nest in a rock cavity or cave entrance on the face of a cliff.

nesting notes

Longest incubation period: Varies, though there's a record of an albatross incubating its egg for 68 days.

Shortest incubation period: Though 12 to 14 days is normal for an American robin, one record shows only seven days before hatching. Hummingbirds require up to 16 days.

Most eggs: If an egg is removed from the nest of a domestic hen every day, she will lay another to replace it, up to 300 eggs a year. Northern flickers will do the same. One flicker laid 71 eggs in 73 days to replace the one egg removed each day.

Most eggs in a single season: Though northern bobwhites normally lay around 20 eggs in a single nest, as many as 40 have been found in one nest, probably laid by two or three hens. Bobwhites and wood ducks are among the few species that will "dump" their eggs in the nests of other hens of the same species.

Killdeer. Many birds build no nests at all. One of the best known of these is the killdeer, which lays four speckled eggs on gravel driveways, stony fields or walkways. When flushed off their eggs, the birds will feign a broken wing to distract the intruder from the eggs. Shortly after the eggs hatch, the chicks follow their parents away from the "nest."

Baltimore oriole. Perhaps the most creative of all nest builders is the female Baltimore oriole. She weaves an intricate 8-inch pouch, attached to twigs high in an elm, maple or willow tree. With the entrance at the top, both parents feed the young by stretching downward into the pouch to reach the open mouths.

Atlantic puffin. This clown-faced shorebird prefers to nest under rocks along the coast of Maine and eastern Canada. (The black guillemot also nests like this.)

Cliff swallow. Though many birds use mud in their nests, only cliff swallows use tiny mud balls to construct globes, resembling adobe houses, attached to cliffs or the sides of buildings. You can find entire colonies nesting side by side in these mud condos.

Brown-headed cowbird. Often dubbed a "lazy bird," this flier lays its eggs in another bird's nest. Here's the history behind the habit: When the bison roamed the great prairies, cowbirds followed the herd to eat the insects the animals attracted or disturbed. To keep up with the moving herd, they laid their eggs in the nests of birds that stayed in one place. As a result of this survival strategy, cowbirds never build their own nests nor raise their own young.

Whip-poor-will. Like its relatives, the whip-poor-will lays its two light-brown eggs on the dead leaves of a forest floor. It's almost impossible to spot these eggs with the naked eye unless you flush the parent from the nest.

Marsh wren. This bird is also a weaver. Marsh wrens weave a sort of glove lashed to standing cattails, reeds or small bushes about 1 to 3 feet above the water. The entrance is on the side, and the inside is tiny compared to the outside dimensions.

Plover. Like terns, plovers lay their eggs on bare, sandy beaches, among seashells that look like the eggs. This strategy helps protect them from the eyes of predators.

FRANCIS & JANICE BERGQUIST

Baltimore oriole

MARIE READ

Great horned owls

Killdeer chick and egg

RICHARD SHIELL

Northern cardinals

winter
wonderland

Create a cold-weather bird haven for your feathered friends in only three easy steps. By David Shaw, Fairbanks, Alaska

I spend a lot of time thinking about winter birds. In Fairbanks, Alaska, where I live, the handful of species that survive the dark winters are forced to deal with extreme cold and short daylight periods.

They are remarkable creatures and are beautifully adapted to their environment. I love them because they remind me, on dark, bitterly cold mornings, that there is life out there in the woods.

Birds, like humans, need only a few things to survive the winter—food, water and shelter—all of which are readily available in the wild. The trick to drawing birds into your yard, though, is to make offerings superior to what they can find elsewhere.

No matter how cold the winters are where you live, here are a few tricks to get the most visitors in your yard.

PHOTOS BY MASLOWSKI WILDLIFE

Food

Quality food is the most important aspect of any bird-friendly backyard. But good bird feeding is, unfortunately, not as straightforward as hanging a feeder in a nearby tree. Here are some things to think about:

Food diversity. Different bird species prefer different types of food. Here in Alaska, black-oil sunflower seeds and peanut butter are sure favorites, while millet will remain uneaten in the feeder. In other parts of the country, the opposite could be true.

Start out by providing a variety of foods to see what your local species prefer. Suet, sunflower seeds, dried and fresh fruit, and even mealworms can make excellent bird food.

Feeder variety. Birds vary their foraging locations. Some, like woodpeckers, prefer to forage while gripping vertically to the side of the tree or feeder. Others, such as chickadees and finches, favor horizontal perches. Juncos and other sparrows often will choose the ground, or flat, platform-style feeders.

Consistency. If you are new to feeding, it may take a few days for birds to find your feeding station, but once they do, they will return again and again. Keeping your feeders full is important. A few days of empty feeders and the birds will quickly disappear for better foraging areas.

Water

Water can be a great way to make your yard stand out. Here are a few things to consider:

Ponds. Birds are accustomed to getting their water from ground-level ponds, puddles and creeks. A small backyard pond with recirculating water is easy to build and is preferred by many birds. If you live in the North, your pond will likely freeze over for winter. But if your area stays above freezing most of the time, a pond is a welcoming addition to any backyard.

Bird baths. These are usually elevated and can seem unnatural for some cautious species. However, baths

Chickadee

FRANCIS & JANICE BERGQUIST

have two notable advantages: ease and the ability to have heated water in winter. Some water is better than none, and heated birdbaths will keep the water unfrozen if your winter temperatures slip below freezing.

Shelter

Shelter is important to birds throughout the year. If you provide protection from weather, cold and predators, your yard will quickly become an appealing place.

Defense. Small birds are hesitant to cross large open areas. This exposes them to predators that may be lurking in the sky above or on the ground below. Avoid this hesitancy by placing your feeders close to trees and shrubs. (Species native to your area will be more appealing than ornamentals.)

Cover. Dense shrubs and trees also provide space for birds to protect themselves from the wind and weather. Evergreens that retain their foliage through the winter are perfect choices. Pines, spruces, junipers or rhododendrons are excellent choices depending on where you live.

Warmth. Where I live in Alaska, one of the biggest challenges facing winter birds is keeping warm. Some species, like the black-capped chickadee, use tree cavities to get out of the cold during the long nights. If you have dead trees where woodpeckers have hollowed out holes, leave them in place. Additionally, chickadees will use old birdhouses or even specially made "roosting boxes." If you live in an extreme environment, consider this addition to your backyard bird habitat.

Sometimes I fool myself into believing that without the food and shelter I provide, "my birds" wouldn't survive the winter. But really, as a scientist and naturalist, I know differently.

If I put my feeders away, the birds would just head back to the forest as they have for millennia. Instead, I do it for me. I feed them because their antics and energy make me smile on brutal winter days. I provide for them because I love the presence of birds.

Blue jay

MASLOWSKI WILDLIFE

berries for birds

By George Harrison, Contributing Editor

Cedar waxwing
in crabapple

Discover the friendly fliers you can attract to your yard in winter.

If it weren't for wild and backyard berries, some of the most familiar birds wouldn't survive the harsh northern winter. The same is true for migrating birds, both those heading south in the fall and those flying north in the spring.

Berries are loaded with carbohydrates, vitamins and sometimes even fats essential to the health of many species. Here are a few common berries and the birds that relish them.

Barberry: Gray catbird, northern mockingbird, brown thrasher.
Chokecherry: Northern cardinal, American robin, cedar waxwing.
Crabapple: Gray catbird, bluebirds, American robin, cedar waxwing.
Highbush cranberry: American robin, bluebirds, northern cardinal.
Manzanita: Northern mockingbird, northern cardinal, cedar waxwing.
Mountain ash: American robin, cedar waxwing, northern cardinal.
Mulberry: Gray catbird, red-bellied woodpecker, titmice, bluebirds, cedar waxwing, northern cardinal, American robin, orioles, tanagers, grosbeaks, doves.
Pagoda dogwood: Northern mockingbird, gray catbird, brown thrasher, northern flicker, downy woodpecker, red-bellied woodpecker, cedar waxwing, oriole, northern cardinal, white-throated sparrow, bluebirds, indigo bunting, kingbirds.
Serviceberry: Gray catbird, northern mockingbird, brown thrasher, northern flicker, downy woodpecker, chickadees, titmice, bluebirds.
Southern wax myrtle: Gray catbird, brown thrasher, northern mockingbird, redbellied woodpecker, chickadees, titmice, bluebirds, yellow-rumped warbler, myrtle warbler, vireos, northern bobwhite.
Spice bush: Gray catbird, wood thrush, veery.
Sweetbay: Red-eyed vireo, American redstart, towhees, American robin, ruffed grouse, wild turkey, northern flicker, pileated woodpecker, great crested flycatcher, blue jay.
Virginia creeper: Gray catbird, northern mockingbird, brown thrasher, downy woodpecker, red-bellied woodpecker, bluebirds, cedar waxwing, chickadee, northern flicker, tree swallow.
Washington hawthorn: Gray catbird, northern mockingbird, northern flicker.
Winterberry: Ruffed grouse, white-throated sparrow, white-crowned sparrow, towhees.

birding in the
big city

Urban dwellers are finding a new way to connect with nature.

By Ellie Martin Cliffe

Craig on his San Francisco balcony

Craig Newmark may be famous for *craigslist.org*, but now he's gaining recognition for something completely different: birding. His busy schedule doesn't leave room for even a bird-watching day trip, but it doesn't have to. After noticing birds in his yard, he installed a bird-watching station on the deck of his San Francisco home office.

"I overlook Sutro Forest, and as a result I get a lot of birds," he says—around 30 species, in fact, including Anna's hummingbirds, western tanagers and Townsend's warblers. "That's a really good reason to depart from work for a moment."

Spread the Word

Thanks to social networking, Craig's hobby has gone public. Tens of thousands of people are tuning in to read bird reports, see photos and watch video posted on his blog (*cnewmark.com*), Twitter feed and Facebook page.

"I'll see one and leap up, grab a camera and go out and try to take a picture," Craig says. "It's fun to share with others, and it feels good to see how many people love birds."

Across the country, city folk are noticing birds during their everyday routines. In Seattle, Ryan Black, a biologist, and Robert Frazier, who works for a non-profit, relish the birdsongs they hear while cultivating their plot at a downtown community garden.

21

"After we're done watering, the birds start calling, waiting for us to leave so they can swoop down from the trees and eat the worms," says Ryan, who has spotted a variety of birds, including robins, American goldfinches and Steller's jays, along with eagles flying overhead. "We can actually see Puget Sound from our garden. It's so picturesque. And the wildlife completes that."

Reconnecting With Nature

So what's the draw of urban birding? "People are craving a reconnection with the simplicity of nature," Ryan says, who suggests it's really easy to do. "That can be accomplished as easily as watching out your window or glancing up as you're walking down the street. It's all around us."

I wholeheartedly agree. When my husband, Ian, and I moved to New York City from rural Wisconsin, I told myself that I'd make time for birding in Central Park, but I became convinced that I'd traded my love of the outdoors for a career. I felt very far from home—until we started getting 6 a.m. wake-up calls from blue jays living in our courtyard.

We hung a feeder from our balcony, curious to see what else we might attract. For weeks the seed was untouched, but one Saturday morning incessant peeping interrupted our breakfast. I rushed to investigate and was delighted to find a female northern cardinal hopping along the railing. The male soon followed. Then other birds—slate-colored juncos, mockingbirds, song sparrows —became regulars, too. Apparently I hadn't strayed from my roots after all.

Now I know that, wherever we are, we birders have something in common. We have taught ourselves how to reconnect, pausing our busy lives to watch birds go about theirs, even if just for a second.

Northern cardinal

urban backyard birding 101

You can create your own backyard oasis, even in the city!

Pick a spot. Select an outdoor space that's easy to see from inside your home. If you live in an apartment, condo or co-op, ask your landlord or the owners association if feeders are allowed.

Set it up. Once you have the OK, choose a tube-style feeder (open ones attract pigeons) and a seed mix to attract many species. Find a sturdy bowl for a birdbath. Replenish seed and water as necessary.

Make a birding kit. Gather a field guide, binoculars (for a larger space), a notebook (aka birding journal) and a pen, and store them near your bird-watching area. Keep a camera or camcorder on hand to get footage of mystery birds so you can identify them later.

Share your experiences. Join a count, like Project FeederWatch, to help collect data for ornithologists. Also post your photos and videos on sites such as *birdsandblooms. com* and *welovebirds.org*.

Mind your p's and q's. Try to be courteous to your neighbors and the birds by removing debris and washing the feeder and birdbath regularly. This will help nix germs and keep the space looking pristine.

on the road

Vacationing? Add one of these top urban birding spots to your itinerary.

Brooklyn, New York
Skip Manhattan's Central Park and visit Prospect Park, where birding lists log more than 200 entries, including American bitterns, green herons and a host of Atlantic migratory birds. 718-287-3400 *prospectpark.org/audubon*

Coral Gables, Florida
Wander along the James A. Kushlan Bird Trail at Fairchild Tropical Botanic Garden and watch for hummingbirds, warblers, herons, buntings and hawks. 305-667-1651, *fairchildgarden.org*

Chicago, Illinois
Jutting out into Lake Michigan, Montrose Point Bird Sanctuary is a pit stop for migrating flocks, plus local species like snowy owls and brown thrashers. 312-742-7529 *chicagoparkdistrict.com*

Houston, Texas
The diverse habitats at Houston Arboretum and Nature Center attract a variety of birds, including tufted titmice and pileated woodpeckers. 713-681-8433 *houstonarboretum.org*

Littleton, Colorado
Look around South Platte Park's ponds and meadows for nearly 100 species, like vesper sparrows, marsh wrens and least flycatchers. 303-730-1022, *sspr.org/nature*

Tucson, Arizona
Get a taste of the Southwest and stop at Sabino Canyon in Coronado National Forest to catch a glimpse of desert species like Gambel's quail, cactus wrens and Scott's orioles. 520-388-8300 *sabinocanyon.org*

Rooftop garden in New York City

Red-headed woodpecker
"Tricolor Beauty"
This stunning black-and-white bird with the completely red head is unmistakable. Sometimes, in the right light, its black feathers can look blue, making it our only red, white and blue bird! Want to impress your friends with an interesting fact? These beauties stash live grasshoppers so tightly into crevices that they cannot escape.

RED-HEADED WOODPECKER IN FLIGHT, ROB CURTIS / THE IMAGE FINDERS; PERCHED, ROLAND JORDAHL.

These fliers are some of the most popular in North America. By Anne Schmauss

All-American Birds

From athletes to plant selections, "all-American" is one of the top honors in the United States. That's why we wanted to put together an all-American bird list from *Birds & Blooms*. While we discovered that it was a bit of a challenge—lots of different opinions!—we finally came up with some top picks, thanks to reader feedback, research, and input from our bird expert, George Harrison.

While this list could have gone on and on, here are the nine all-Americans that we settled on. Take a look!

"The Acrobat"

White-breasted nuthatch

If you see a bird moving headfirst down a trunk of a tree, it's probably a white-breasted nuthatch. By approaching tree bark from this angle, the agile nuthatch finds bugs and larvae that other birds moving upward or side to side may have missed.

American robin

No bird symbolizes the beginning of spring like the American robin—even though many do overwinter even in the coldest parts of the

"The Early Bird"

country. They just start to show themselves more on your lawn when warm weather and earthworms surface. In the winter, robins flock together in treetops and around berry-producing shrubs and trees. Planting native, berry-producing shrubs and trees may help attract robins to your yard all year.

Also, robins love to bathe, so a birdbath gives them another reason to stick close to home.

Black-capped chickadee

This high-energy, cute little bird loves to grab a seed from a bird feeder and go elsewhere to eat it, often making dozens of trips back and forth. This popular bird is loved for its perky, friendly nature and good looks. Named from its

Bluebirds

The fall and rise of the bluebird follows the story of America itself. Flocks of bluebirds used to be common across the United States, but as Americans migrated across the continent, much of the prairie was transformed and the population diminished. There is a happy ending, though. In the 1960s, bluebird lovers began sounding the alarm, encouraging people to put out bluebird boxes. Through the conservation efforts of thousands of bird lovers, the bluebird has truly made a comeback.

chickadee-dee-dee call, chickadees are very common at feeders and love black-oil sunflower seed. With enough time and patience, you can even teach them to feed directly from your hand!

"Little But Lovely"

Ruby-throated hummingbird

Americans love the determination and beauty of the ruby-throated hummingbird. This tiny bird migrates north from Mexico and Central America by flying 500 miles across the Gulf of Mexico. After their amazing 20-hour journey, they are exhausted and hungry. Ruby-throated hummingbirds are widespread throughout the Midwest and East and are easily attracted with a sugar-water feeder.

"Friendliest"

"The Comeback Kid"

Readers from our Facebook page chime in to answer the question: What defines an American bird to you?

A **mockingbird**. I just love to hear them sing.　—SUSAN ROOKS

I love **chickadees** because they are tame enough to eat from my feeder while I'm filling it.　—SHERI WINELAND

I love **house wrens**. They are so trusting, building their nests right by my back door.　—JANET FULMER

Goldfinches! Their sunny yellow color brightens my day.
　—CHARLENE ESTES CUSUMANO

I love **hummingbirds**. They are such tiny things with so much energy.
　—GESILA HARGROVE

I love **cardinals** with their standout color all four seasons of the year.
　—JAN FAULKENDER SALISBURY

I love **ravens** because of their resourcefulness and willingness to get the job done. Americans have done this from the infancy of our nation.
　—SARA CARLSON

Eagles are beautiful and majestic. It makes me proud to be an American.
　—JADE W. RICHARDSON

My favorite bird is the **purple martin**. They're beautiful and have an unusual song, and most people don't know much about them.　—CHERYL WYRICK

I love, love, love to see the **pileated woodpeckers**. They're red, white and black—not far from red, white and blue.　—NANCY ESSNER JACKSON

NUTHATCH: MARIE READ; ROBIN, ROLAND JORDAHL; RUBY-THROATED HUMMINGBIRD; BLUEBIRDS: MASLOWSKI WILDLIFE; CHICKADEE, AL MASON

Northern cardinal

The northern cardinal is the state bird of a whopping seven states! Because the male cardinal keeps his bright feathers throughout the winter, one can spot this stunning bird even on the coldest of days. Here's another fun fact—most female birds don't sing, but the female cardinal does. She sings mostly while on the nest, so maybe she's telling her mate to bring dinner!

"Best Looks"

My favorite is **cedar waxwings**. There's just something about them with their sleek bandit "masks."

—LAURA JOHNSON

This is like deciding between your children! But I think I'll go with the **western scrub-jay** because it's beautiful, smart and talented.

—JANIS KNIGHT

The **bluebird** is my favorite bird. It seems American to me because it has blue and white on it, just like the flag.

—JONELLE BRANDT GIDZINSKI

I'll vote for **robins**. I love their songs, and they bring spring with them!

—SYLVIA BARBERO LEVY

Talk to Us! Is your favorite missing from the list? Discover more great birds on the "Most Wanted" section of *birdsandblooms.com*.

Hey, Canada!
We didn't forget you!

The national bird of Canada is the common loon. This amazing flier impresses many birdwatchers with its diving habits. It will be swimming on a lake and then will suddenly dive down to catch fish.

American goldfinch

American goldfinches almost never eat insects, relying heavily on seed. Americans love this gorgeous finch because of the male's vibrant yellow plumage in spring. They are easy to attract to bird feeders, though they do have more expensive tastes, preferring nyger seed.

"The Golden Touch"

Bald eagle

This magnificent bird, named the symbol of our country in 1792, was on the verge of extinction just 40 years ago because of the pesticide DDT. When eagles eat fish and other DDT-contaminated food, they become contaminated. The ban on DDT and the strict protection of the bald eagle have resulted in its resurgence. The bird is now widespread throughout the nation and was removed from the endangered species list in 2007—a true American conservation story.

"Amazing Survivor"

Cry for Attention

We took this picture one spring behind our house. A pileated woodpecker pair was raising its family in this tree. What a racket those two nestlings would make when their parents showed up to feed them. In this photo, I can imagine they're saying, "Hey, Mama! Did you bring us dinner?"

—MARCIE SULLIVAN
Peterborough, Ontario

Golden Technique

I first learned about this photo technique in an old issue of *Birds & Blooms*. A simple tube lined with reflective film lets you experiment with special effects.

At first I focused on shooting flowers this way, but then I expanded to birds and butterflies.

For this photo, I captured an American goldfinch at a feeder. I put my camera on a tripod close to the feeder, then sat about 30 feet away, holding a shutter wire. I really like how the photo turned out!

—SHARON LA REAU, *Janesville, Wisconsin*

Look Both Ways

A few months ago, I was waiting for the light to change at a busy intersection when I noticed an ibis walking across the street. The bird made it safely across, waited for the light to change and then proceeded to cross the other street.

I wish I'd had my camera! Why the ibis didn't just fly across, I have no idea. But it was truly an amazing sight. It just made my day! —**JAMES DALLMANN**
West Melbourne, Florida

Resident in Waiting

On the first warm day in early April, I was high up on a ladder hanging my birdhouses. I had one in hand when an eastern bluebird flew right up to me. Then it flew away in a flourish of bright blue and settled in a tree just a few yards away.

The bluebird watched me as I hurried to hang the house and move the ladder away from the area. As soon as I was out of the way, that bird didn't waste any time. It immediately claimed the birdhouse as its own! —**MOLLY KLEIN**
Cedar Lake, Indiana

Hard at Work

I was fascinated to watch a red-headed woodpecker (right) make a hole in a tree for her family one day. First she'd drill for about five minutes. Then she would come to the opening and make loud screeching noises. I think she was calling for her mate to come help her.

He never came, though. So she kept retreating back into the hole to do more work. Every little while she'd come out with a mouthful of shavings and then spit them out. This entire process lasted about two hours, and I really enjoyed it. —**LUANNE BROOKER**
Sandersville, Georgia

Unexpected Photo Op

I was walking around Lake Catherine in Palos Heights, a Chicago suburb, with camera in hand when something captured my eye. I saw a mother duck fly off from a spot near a waterfall, so I went over to take a closer look. I was surprised to see these ducklings (below) hiding beneath the waterfall and looking up at me from amid the bubbles! —**LINDA MALMBORG**
Mokena, Illinois

bird tales

Eyes of Blue

I was very excited to come across two anhingas in my neighborhood a couple of years ago. Although I was able to photograph only one of them, the picture intrigued me.

The bird's eye was bright blue, unlike anything I had ever seen. At first, I thought that it was just the setting on my camera. But after a little research online, I discovered that when anhingas are in their breeding plumage, they have a blue ring around their eyes. I'm glad I captured the moment.

—RITA AMBERGE, *Sunrise, Florida*

Hair Today, Nest Tomorrow

My husband, Rich, was sitting on the back porch swing, and I was in the kitchen looking out the window while doing dishes. I watched as a tufted titmouse flew in and perched on a chair before landing on my husband's head. The titmouse pulled out some of Rich's hair and flew away.

The bird, which showed no fear, came back seven times to pull more hair. Rich wishes he could find the nest that was built from his hair!

—DORIS VICKROY
Hummelstown, Pennsylvania

Bluebird Huddle

During a recent January ice storm, trees cracked or fell down all around us. Every time my wife and I heard this, I'd go outside to survey the damage.

Once, heading back inside, I noticed something white on the porch floor. I shone a light down and saw bird droppings, then looked up and saw a group of eastern bluebirds up high.

The birds were all huddled togeth-er and fluffed out against the miserable weather. I went back inside to get my camera and then took this picture (below). The bluebirds returned every night for the rest of the week.

—KEN DECKER, *Springfield, Missouri*

Dumpster Diving

Nearly every spring, a couple of wrens make their nest next to the air conditioner in the window at the front

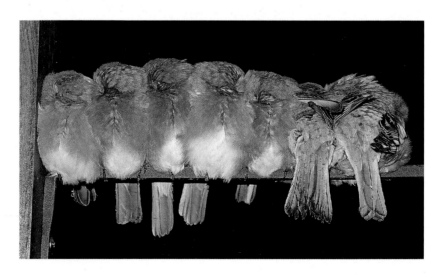

By Ellie Martin Cliffe

My love affair with owls bloomed slowly.
In fact, until recently, they terrified me—
I wanted to be nowhere near their hooked
beaks, sharp talons and wide eyes. My phobia
peaked when I shared a campsite with a family of
eastern screech-owls and imagined that an attack
was imminent. But a certain book about young
wizards with pet owls piqued my curiosity, and I
soon became completely enamored of these birds.

1 2

Great horned owl

Owls live on every continent except Antarctica. What's more, from France to Australia, many of our ancestors were intrigued enough to include wise or ominous owls in their legends. No matter what role they've played in human minds, owls have led a secret life all their own—until now. We're setting the record straight.

MYTH 1 – *all owls are nocturnal.*

Although horror movies suggest that owls are active exclusively at night, this just isn't the case. Some, including great gray and northern hawk owls, are diurnal, meaning they're awake during the day. If food is scarce, owls hunt around the clock. In times of plenty, they cache their prey by stashing extra in or around nests.

MYTH 2 – *male and female owls are identical.*

Plumage is the same in most species, but some variations occur. Female snowy and barn owls have more dark spots than the males. Size is another story. Females are almost always bigger than males, surpassing them by as much as 40 percent in some species. The reason is a bit of a mystery, but most ornithologists agree that a bigger body allows for better nest protection as well as greater egg production.

MYTH 3 – *owls see in complete darkness.*

Huge eyes do make for excellent vision in low light, but owls can't see in the dark. Generally, diurnal owls use their eyesight more than nocturnal ones, and for most, sight is secondary to hearing. An owl's facial disk, resembling a satellite dish with funnellike indentations around each eye, helps channel the quietest of sounds to its ears. Once the owl pinpoints the prey's location, it stealthily flies toward the sound, adjusting its flight path to accommodate obstacles and keeping its face pointed at its destination. Then, snap! The owl's talons lock around its next meal.

MYTH 4 – *owls hate water.*

In reality, many species have been observed bathing and drinking in streams and lakes, and some smaller ones have even been spotted in birdbaths. Waterlogged feathers can make flying difficult, so, like most birds, owls are armed with a gland that releases a protective oily substance, distributed while preening.

MYTH 5 – *all owls live in the woods.*

While many species do live in forests, several species—short-eared and snowy owls included—make their homes

GROWING UP. In this photo of snowy owls, the two on the left are juveniles. You can tell by their extra spots and markings. The owl on the right is an adult. The juveniles will get their adult coloring sometime after their first year.

4

Great gray owl

3

Great gray owl

5

Burrowing owls

in more open landscapes. Grassland-dwelling burrowing owls are the single North American species that actually lives underground. Some owls aren't particular about where they nest: Elf owls take up residence in cacti, agave stalks and even utility poles, while barn owls roost in a variety of buildings. Of course, habitat determines diet, too, so although rodents are the most popular prey, owls also hunt insects, fish, reptiles and other birds.

Lesson Learned

My concern about being attacked wasn't completely off base. Owls can be quite territorial. Luckily, learning how to respect them is all it takes to avoid a run-in. On future camping trips, I'll welcome the sounds of owls in the trees, though I'll sleep best if they—and their dinners—stay a few sites away.

backyard birding solutions

Squirrels, bluebirds and cats are among our most frequent topics for questions. George offers his advice. By George Harrison

Combating Squirrels

Sure, squirrels have to eat, too, but you don't want them gobbling your bird-seed supply in just a few short hours. Here are my top five tips to keep squirrels away from your feeders.

● Squirrel baffles above and below bird feeders work well if you follow the rule of 5-7-9: If the feeder is 5 feet above the ground, 7 feet from the nearest tree or building and 9 feet below an overhang, squirrels should not be able to reach it.

● To keep squirrels and raccoons from eating suet cakes, sprinkle the cakes with cayenne pepper. Birds can't taste or smell the way mammals do. After just one lick, the squirrels should go running for water, but the pepper won't bother your birds.

● If you want to hang a bird feeder from a wire, string at least half a dozen 1-liter soda bottles on each side. Just punch a hole in the bottom of each bottle and thread the wire through it to the bottle's open top. Squirrels may try to run across the spinning bottles, but after falling enough times they will give up.

● Use chicken wire to build an enclo-sure around any feeder to allow birds but not squirrels to reach the food.

● Squirrels love sunflower seeds in any form. If you feed the birds other seeds, such as safflower and nyjer, the squir-rels should show far less interest.

Attracting Bluebirds

Want to attract bluebirds to your backyard? It's easier than you think, and the rewards are definitely worth the effort. Here are my top five tips for success:

● Bluebirds love eating live mealworms more than any other feeder food. You can buy them by the hundreds or thousands from pet stores. If you offer a handful of mealworms on a tray feeder out in the open where the bluebirds can see them, they should come for dinner. Feed them once in the morning and once in the early evening.

● Bluebirds are cavity nesters and will readily move into a birdhouse on the edge of a field or open lawn. They prefer houses that are 5½ inches by 5½ inches by 10 inches high, colored in light earthy tones. The entrance hole should be 1½ inches, centered 6 inches above the floor, and mounted on a post 5 to 10 feet above the ground, facing the open area.

● Both house sparrows and tree swallows are likely to try to nest in bluebird houses, often by evicting bluebirds. A second house, located nearby, may satisfy everyone.

● As winters have become warmer, bluebirds have been staying on their nesting grounds all year. The same houses that were used for nesting in summer are excellent roosting cavities in winter. Some people have found more than a dozen at a time roosting in one house.

● Bluebirds regularly use birdbaths to drink and bathe. If the water is moving and splashing, you're even more likely to entice them.

Bird-Watching for Cats

Like all members of my family, Lucy, our rescued shelter cat, is a birdwatcher. She spends most of her waking moments at one of our four windows where feeders are easy to see.

There is a continuing disagreement among cat owners over the merits of keeping cats indoors. Those opposed believe that cats are meant to have free range of the outdoors. Those in favor believe that indoor cats are healthier, happier and safer and will enjoy a longer life.

Much research has shown how detrimental free-ranging cats are to certain kinds of birds, especially grassland birds. Some species, including bobolinks, meadowlarks, dickcissels and several sparrows, are actually threatened with extinction from environmental problems that include free-ranging cats. Here are a couple of things to consider in the interest of both your pet cat and the birds in your backyard.

● First of all, by keeping your cat indoors, you are offering it a healthier, happier and longer life while saving the lives of birds that frequent your feeders, as well as the lives of ducklings and other baby birds that hatch in your neighborhood.

● To keep your indoor cat from being bored when you are away, set up bird feeders, a birdbath and birdhouses near windows where it will be entertained.

● The birds quickly get used to the face on the other side of the glass. It's a win-win solution for both the cat and the birds.

Northern cardinal
Photo by Maslowski Wildlife

Tufted titmouse
Finalist in our Backyard Photo Contest
Photo by Doris Dumrauf

Northern flicker nestlings
Photo by Maslowski Wildlife

Eastern bluebird
Photo by reader Ted Rose

Red-bellied woodpecker
Richard Day / Daybreak Imagery

KATE BALDWIN

CHAPTER 2

Budget
Backyards

A beautiful and bird-friendly backyard doesn't need to break the bank. These budget tips, low-cost plant picks and do-it-yourself project ideas will leave more money in your wallet.

Hidden Treasures **44**

Top 10: Best Value Plants **50**

Budget Gardening & Birding Tips **55**

For Less **56**

Did You Know? **63**

Top 10: Annuals from Seed **64**

Golf-club trellis.

Did you treat yourself to new golf clubs this year? Don't throw out your retired set! Use three clubs as a trellis to support vining plants, or as an accent in the garden. Simply wrap copper wire tightly around the handles of all three clubs, at the base of the club heads. Bury the handles in your container or flower bed next to the plants you want to train to grow up the trellis.

Projects by Amy Duncan,
Beth Evans-Ramos
and Lisa Hilderbrand
Photos by Kate Baldwin

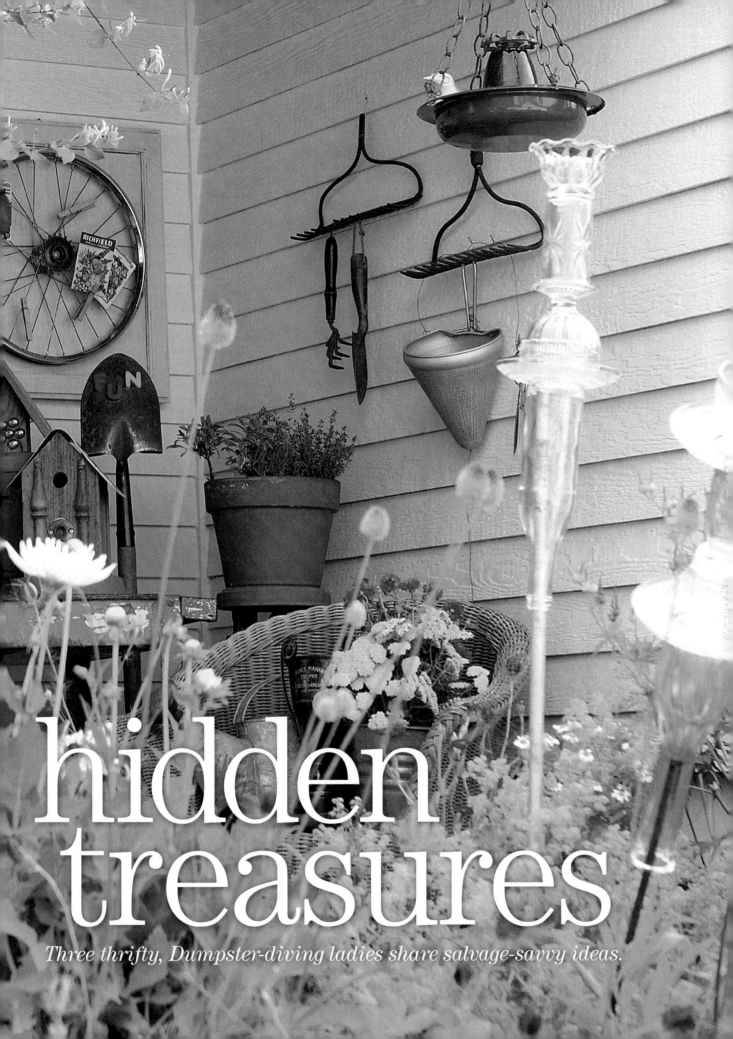

hidden treasures

Three thrifty, Dumpster-diving ladies share salvage-savvy ideas.

These days it pays to be a bargain hunter. What's even more rewarding is finding those hidden treasures that other people consider trash—for free!

Join Amy Duncan, Beth Evans–Ramos and Lisa Hilderbrand on the eco-journey that led them to create the Salvage Studio in Washington, a showcase of inspiring home and garden items made from recycled materials and found items.

"It seems that people throw away so much because they can't think of alternative uses," says Amy. "Our projects redefine the adage 'One person's trash is another's treasure.'"

The next time you pass a thrift store or flea market or are simply cleaning out the attic, take a moment to see if there's hidden potential in any of your trash. You just might find quirky garden decor waiting to be discovered.

Mailbox planter. If your mailbox can hardly hold letters anymore, turn it on its side and transform it into a planter for flowers. Remember to include drainage holes, and plant it with your favorite spring bulbs or another colorful container combination.

Garden goddesses. Think your garden deserves a trophy? Even if your garden hasn't won any awards, adorn it with some rescued trophy tops displayed in a flower bed. Attach rusted metal washers, a garden-hose nozzle or other odds and ends, and your trophies become quirky garden statues.

Barn-wood bench. Looking for a unique garden bench to use as a focal point? Look no further than an old set of metal furniture. A weathered piece of wood placed on three chairs makes a statement against a fence, shed or house.

For more ideas on home and garden inspiration, pick up a copy of *The Salvage Studio: Sustainable Home Comforts to Organize, Entertain and Inspire* (Skipstone, $21.95).

Looking for a rare item, or stuff that someone is willing to give away? Try *craigslist. org* or *freecycle.org*. You'll be amazed at what you might find on these websites. But be forewarned: Free stuff goes fast!

Bicycle-wheel organizer. Tack your to-do list or other odds and ends to an old bike wheel. It's a fun way to look at your chores, since the wheel can still spin—it will cheer you up to give them a whirl or two. Wooden clothespins work well to secure items to the spokes.

Lampshade birdbath. Give new life to an antique lamp fixture and keep birds happy, too. Make sure to safely remove all electrical cords and the socket from the lamp base, and then place a glass ceiling-lamp globe upside down on top. Make sure to secure it with hardware so that it won't leak, and wait for the birds to enjoy their new bath.

Garden dish towers. Check the back of your own cupboards or Grandma's for old china or glass dishes (but leave the prized antiques!). When stacked high, they become a beautiful garden tower. Arrange your dishes first, and when you find a combination that works, secure them with clear, waterproof glue.

If a pot, saucer or other item has a little rust on it, don't toss it! The "rust"-ic charm makes it perfect for the garden.

Sedum

1

best value plants

Get more bang for your buck with these reliable garden favorites.

By Stacy Tornio

When you're at the garden store, the cost of plants can add up in a hurry. Before you know it, you're spending $100, $200 and more on plants that you hope will work in your backyard.

Beautiful and reliable plants don't have to be a gamble, though. Plus, you can even save money in the long run if you know what you're looking for.

The 10 perennials on our list will be back year after year, will save you money on watering (all are drought-tolerant!) and will eventually fill up a lot of space. So the next time you're thinking about adding to your garden, stretch your dollar a little further and let our best-value plant list be your guide.

Agastache **2**

Coreopsis **3**

Pasque flower **4**

Hens-and-chicks **5**

Yucca **6**

Yarrow **7**

Penstemon **8**

Ornamental grass **9**

Lantana **10**

1

Sedum

(*Sedum* species, Zones 3 to 10)

You rarely have to worry about whether this perennial will come back each year. One of the most reliable growers around, it offers delightful color well into fall. The star-shaped blooms are a treat for butterflies, and fall-blooming varieties offer fuel to monarchs and other late fliers on their journey south.

Why we love it: It's one of the first perennials to emerge in spring, and then it offers interesting foliage until it begins blooming from late summer through the end of fall.

2

Agastache

(*Agastache* species, Zones 5 to 11)

This drought-tolerant perennial often gets forgotten, but it's the perfect addition to any wildlife habitat, with flowers that attract hummingbirds and butterflies all summer long. Late in the season, the seed heads provide food for birds. You can choose just about any flower color you want, with cultivars offering orange, pink, red, purple and blue blooms.

Why we love it: The tall blooms offer a great backdrop to just about any perennial or annual you add to the landscape.

5

Hens-and-chicks

(*Sempervivum tectorum*, Zones 3 to 8)

We love this tough plant with its clusters of rosette-shaped leaves. It seems to have limitless possibilities: Grow it in unusual shallow containers (like a pair of old high-heeled shoes!) or in rocky, challenging spaces. Newer cultivars are better than ever, so check them out at the garden center.

Why we love it: It's very forgiving. It can go days without water, then it perks right back up once you remember.

6

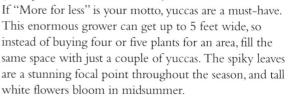

Yucca

(*Yucca filamentosa*, Zones 4 to 10)

If "More for less" is your motto, yuccas are a must-have. This enormous grower can get up to 5 feet wide, so instead of buying four or five plants for an area, fill the same space with just a couple of yuccas. The spiky leaves are a stunning focal point throughout the season, and tall white flowers bloom in midsummer.

Why we love it: The foliage lasts all season, so the blooms are just a bonus.

9

Ornamental grass

Never underestimate the power of grasses. They are the perfect garden backdrop, adding texture, color and fullness to any space. Look for switchgrass (*Panicum virgatum*, Zones 3 to 9) for splendid fall color and also feather reed grass (*Calamagrostis* x *acutiflora*) for a stately sweep up to 5 feet. Ask local garden center experts for a grass recommendation, too, since they'll know what works best in your area.

Why we love it: It doesn't matter what your style is, there's an ornamental grass to fit any garden space.

10

Lantana

(*Lantana camara*, Zones 8 to 11)

What a beauty this abundant bloomer is! While it's really considered a perennial only in warmer regions, you can keep this lovely plant going by using it in containers and then overwintering it indoors. If you're successful, you'll have a garden all-star for years to come.

Why we love it: The compact cluster of blooms has a tropical feel, and butterflies love it.

3 Coreopsis

(*Coreopsis* species, Zones 3 to 9)
Though you can also find this bloom as an easy annual to grow from seed, make sure you pick up the perennial version, too. It loves the sun and thrives in dry conditions. New varieties offer pretty alternatives to the traditional yellow blooms, and the orange, pink and bright-red varieties add a color twist to this favorite.
Why we love it: Nothing beats the heat like this tough beauty. It just keeps going and going and ...

4 Pasque flower

(*Pulsatilla vulgaris*, Zones 4 to 8)
If you're a gardener who appreciates unique blooms, it's time you made room for pasque flowers. Early-spring bloomers, mostly with purple blossoms, they add an element of texture to your garden. While it's not the first perennial many gardeners think of, the drought-tolerant, easy-care pasque flower definitely deserves top honors.
Why we love it: Once the flowers are gone, attractive ornamental seed heads last for several weeks.

7 Yarrow

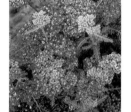

(*Achillea* species, Zones 3 to 9)
What's not to love about this perennial? It can grow in almost any condition, it blooms all the way until frost, and it offers lovely color both in the garden and as a cut flower. Now all you have to decide is which cultivar to grow! Moonshine has light-yellow blooms; Red Velvet offers a nice strawberry-pink alternative. Just pick one that is not too aggressive, and you'll be on the road to success.
Why we love it: Though yarrow is sometimes considered a weed, the right cultivar is like discovering hidden treasure!

8 Penstemon

(*Penstemon* species and cultivars, Zones 3 to 8)
Don't let the delicate tubular blooms of penstemon fool you. This plant is tough, blooming early summer to fall. The signature perennial is mostly known for its scarlet flowers, but you can also find cultivars in purple, white and pink. For a distinctive look, try Husker Red, which sports reddish foliage and pinkish-white blooms.
Why we love it: With its red, tube-shaped blooms, it's easy to see why it's a hummingbird favorite.

Best-Value Blooms for Birds

These blooms offer seeds for your feathered friends long after they stop blooming!

Liatris
Stokesia
Amaranth
Joe Pye weed
Purple coneflower
Hollyhock
Black-eyed Susan

Backyard Bargains
from our experts

Save some cash with these frugal gardening and birding tips from contributing experts Melinda Myers and George Harrison.

Gardening tips from Melinda:

● **Use what's in your yard.** It's good for the environment and the budget. I shred and use my leaves as mulch. I also use landscape trimmings to create trellises or wattle fences.

● **Leave the grass clippings on the lawn.** A season's worth of clippings is equal to one fertilization.

● **Buy quality tools.** That $9 trowel not only outlasts the cheaper ones, you're less likely to lose it if you spent more for it.

● **Use what is at hand to solve garden problems.** A trip to the basement, sewing area or garage can usually turn up something to use in the garden. Leftover jute from my macramé days comes in handy and adds a bit of color when tying up tomatoes. I save the twist ties from packaging as well. Plastic buckets from my cat's litter make great containers, weed buckets and stackable storage for potting soil, fertilizer and birdseed.

● **Water wisely.** I make sure plants have sufficient water during the first season or two as they get established. And when you do water, do so thoroughly and less frequently overall.

● **Let nature take care of most things in the garden.** Overuse and improper use of chemicals disrupts nature's balance. I like to let lady beetles, praying mantises and green lacewings help keep my garden pests under control.

Birding tips from George:

● **Easy scoop.** An empty plastic gallon milk bottle, cut in the form of a scoop with a handle on top, costs nothing and works well for filling seed feeders.

● **Instant feeder.** Along the same lines, if you cut feed ports from a milk jug and then hang it from a string, you'll have an instant feeder.

● **Simple suet.** If you know a deer hunter, ask for the throwaway white suet. It makes perfect bird food.

● **Homemade nectar.** You'll see nectar mixes in the store, but don't waste your money. Mix your own formula from 1 part sugar to 4 parts water. This works for both hummingbirds and orioles—and you don't need to add food coloring for either one.

● **Protect your bounty.** Don't let critters get into your stored seed. Just store in a metal garbage can with a lid and place bricks on top. It's a simple way to critter-proof your supply.

● **Dryer vent baffle.** An aluminum dryer vent—or even a child's Slinky—over a post will keep squirrels from climbing up to the feeder.

● **Critter control.** A sprinkle of cayenne pepper on suet will keep raccoons and squirrels away, but not birds because they can't smell or taste.

for less

Save money in your backyard with these reader secrets.

Grow a Living Wreath

Make a living piece of art by planting a wreath made of succulents! These wreaths are easy to maintain and can go weeks without water in some environments. Hang them indoors or out in most climates, and they'll be a hit with your guests.

Patti Smith of Apache Junction, Arizona, makes and sells these at her online Etsy store, *succulentdesigns.etsy.com*. She uses a wire wreath frame, moss and succulent cuttings for her wreaths.

Best Succulents for Wreaths:

Aeonium

Crassula

Echeveria

Graptopetalum

Kalanchoe

Sedum (low-growing or trailing)

Sempervivum

Senecio

X Pachyveria

cheap eats

Want to attract birds for pennies? It's easy. Just plant these annuals from seed in spring. By late summer, they'll be a plentiful food source for seed-eating birds.

Sunflower

Cosmos

Bachelor's button

Cleome

Dahlberg daisy

Mexican sunflower

Black-eyed Susan

Orioles *in an Instant*

You don't need a special feeder to invite orioles to your yard this spring. Just take an old suet cage feeder and fill it with oranges instead. The orioles will love this special treat!

Try putting grapes or berries in a suet feeder to see what feathered friends you can attract.

the need for seed

Get ready for nesting season with these clever seed eggs! Angie Dixon from Blaine, Washington, has mastered this technique and sells the eggs on her website, *oopsiedaisydesign.net*. To try these yourself, just follow Angie's simple recipe.

⅓ cup gelatin
1½ cups water
8 cups birdseed

Mix gelatin and water over low heat until the gelatin is melted and clear. Remove from heat and stir in birdseed. Stir until there is no dry seed. Form mixture into egg shapes. Refrigerate for two to four hours and dry on baking rack for three days.

Seed starting *made easy*

These suburban moms drive minivans, raise chickens and know how to make magic out of newspapers. By Deanna Carter and Daisy Siskin

You don't need a fancy kit or special pots to start your own seeds. All you need are some newspapers and a little tape. Then you'll have dozens of biodegradable pots ready for your favorite plants. Here's how to make them:

1. Take a sheet of newspaper and cut it in half and then fourths. (You might try cutting several layers at once to save time, but use only one layer per pot.)

2. Take a small round container (we used a spice jar). Roll the paper around it, leaving about an inch of overhang at one end. Don't roll it too tightly, or it will be hard to get the jar out later.

3. Fold the overhang in, as if you were wrapping a present. Then seal with tape. (Masking tape is more biodegradable than other kinds.)

4. Remove the jar and then fold in the edges all around the top. This helps with stability and gives you a shorter pot.

5. Repeat until you have all the pots you want!

1-2

3

4

10 More Uses for Newspaper

1. Cover the soil surrounding your plants with four layers of newspaper before adding mulch in spring. This will control weeds.

2. Add shreds of paper to a compost pile to increase air circulation and add nutrients.

3. Instead of digging up sod for a new bed, just build on the current foundation by putting down at least four overlapping layers of newspaper. This will essentially compost your existing lawn.

4. Stuff an old mesh onion bag with shreds of newspaper and hang outside for birds to pluck for nesting material.

5. Line your compost pails with a layer or two of newspaper instead of buying expensive liners.

6. Make kitchen cleanup a snap by lining your counters with a couple of layers of newspaper to catch vegetable peelings.

7. Mix shreds of newspaper with dryer lint for kindling.

8. Prevent the spread of rot when ripening tomatoes by wrapping each fruit in newspaper. Then store in a cool, dark place.

9. Save your excess newspaper and donate to a local animal shelter.

10. Reseed bare lawn patches and protect through germination with a half-and-half mixture of seeds and newspaper shreds. Simply moisten the mixture and spread in bare spots.

Be environmentally friendly and go easy on your pocketbook at the same time. "Green" ideas are typically budget-friendly, too!

Recycled Glass Feeder

We love artists who use recycled materials to help out our feathered friends. Dawn Frame of Lake Charles, Louisiana, made this feeder out of recycled glass. If you have vintage glass on hand, try assembling your own bird feeder using silicone auto or marine glue. Dawn shares these tips:

- Inspect your glass carefully for cracks, chips and water spots. Using imperfect glassware is fine, but you might end up with a hazy or crooked feeder.
- Do all gluing outdoors or in a well-ventilated area.
- Hang your bird feeder with braided galvanized picture wire and top it off with acrylic beads.
- Make sure the glue and glassware are dishwasher safe. Then you can just pop your feeders in the dishwasher if the birds make a mess of them.

Check out Dawn's recycled glass feeders at dframe102868.etsy.com.

press, frame & save

Keep your favorite flower long after it blooms by pressing it and preserving it in a frame. Sandy Zuidersma from Moline, Michigan, made and framed this cardinal flower. She presses flowers all the time for her online store, Flowers, Fleurs, Flores (check it out at *flowersfleursflores.etsy.com*).

This is a sweet way to make cards, bookmarks, gift tags or anything else you can think of.

flower pressing tips from Sandy

- Choose newly bloomed flowers.
- Sandwich blossoms between sheets of blotting paper, then between sheets of newspaper.
- Press newspaper under books with heavy weights (such as bricks) on top.
- For best results, press blooms for six to eight weeks.
- When you're ready to decorate with your pressings, try using a fine paintbrush or tweezers to position flower before gluing.

Grow microgreens

Learn a money-saving secret to harvesting crops in 10 days from this thrifty mom. By Daisy Siskin

If you're an impatient gardener like me, microgreens might just be your thing. Microgreens are vegetable and herb plants grown only to the stage of their first few baby leaves. Super-high in nutrients, they're harvested by snipping the stems just above the soil and are enjoyed in a variety of dishes— often in upscale restaurants.

When they're available in supermarkets at all, prices are eye-popping, so growing your own is the way to go. Fortunately, it's criminally easy to do. All you need are seeds, soilless planting mix, a container, a fork and a spray bottle. Here's how you do it:

1. Purchase a packet of a microgreens blend or select individual packets and blend your own. Good choices include lettuce, arugula, broccoli, celery, radish, beet, chard, herbs and Asian greens.

2. Moisten the soilless mix in a separate container, blending well to allow the water to be absorbed.

3. Clear-lidded plastic containers make excellent mini-greenhouses. Poke a couple of ventilation holes in the top. Fill about 1 inch deep with the moist planting medium. Use the fork to smooth the surface.

4. Sow the seeds about ⅛ inch to ¼ inch apart. Gently tamp down the seeds with your fingers.

5. Mist the seeds with the sprayer and close the container or cover with plastic wrap. Place in a sunny window and wait. You may see some activity as soon as the next day.

1

3

4-5

6. Mist with water as the planting medium begins to feel dry. When the plants have a few leaves, take your scissors and harvest the tiny bounty. Rinse gently and store as you would lettuce in a crisper.

Eating Microgreens

Enjoy your microgreens with these suggestions:

- Toss with a subtly flavored vinaigrette and serve over fresh mozzarella and slices of heirloom tomatoes.

- Use as an artistic topknot atop a tender filet.

- Mix into a salad of tender lettuce for extra zing and interest.

- Garnish canapés and other appetizers for a party.

- Add to sandwiches instead of alfalfa sprouts.

Garden Glass Art

Susan Engel of Schuyler, Nebraska, is a pro at turning scrap glass pieces into garden art. Just take a look at some of her creations, and learn a few of her secrets at the same time.

1. Bench. Cut the glass shapes, place them in a mold and then pour concrete over the glass. Buy the legs from a concrete supply company.

2. Garden stake. Once you have a starting shape, use scrap glass, nuggets and stone to decorate.

3. Gazing ball. This art piece started with a bowling ball. Add mosaic glass pieces to customize your design.

4. Birdbath. Glue two terra-cotta base trays together, a small one inside a large one. Then mosaic them with glass pieces, nuggets and flowers. Grout and seal to keep it from fading.

Create your own garden art

with an old, leaky birdbath. Instead of throwing it out, add some soil and succulents. You'll have an instant container and an attractive addition to your garden!

Containers for cheap

Readers share their recycled container ideas.

My son used to love playing with these trucks, but he has grown up—and I found another use for them. They're a playful way to display the smaller planters in my garden (right).

—**PATTI FETTERS**, *Uncasville, Connecticut*

My front porch needed a planter, so I found an old fireplace grate that used to be in my husband's grandmother's farmhouse in 1947. This antique (far right) displays my flowers while helping us remember our loved ones.

—**ELLEN EASTTY**, *Millington, New Jersey*

When our granddaughters visited us one summer, we made a rocking chair garden together (below). My husband dug the old chair out of a Dumpster, and I painted it and added their names. They picked out the flowers and planted them. It was fun to share gardening with them.

—**LINDA BROWN**, *Germantown, Ohio*

I loved the tipsy pots idea that I've seen other readers contribute to the magazine. This is my version (right) of double tipsy pots! I love the colors of the pots, and the birds seem to love them as well. —**PAT GRUWELL** *Grass Valley, California*

did you know?

You can save hundreds of dollars in your backyard!

$70
On average, a family will spend $70 a year to grow their own veggies— and then they will harvest about $600 worth of produce!

$23
You can save an average of $23 per ton by composting your own yard waste and avoiding collection costs.

1+2=FREE
One part plant-based kitchen scraps plus two parts dead leaves equals healthy free compost.

30%

When you water your lawn at midday, you'll lose 30% of that water to evaporation. Instead, water early in the morning to make the most out of your water and reduce your bill!

66%

You can save an estimated 66% by buying small plants and cultivating them instead of buying plants that are already grown.

$0
The amount of cash you'll spend on solar lighting after the initial purchase of equipment.

$10
Average amount you can save per shrub by planting your own instead of hiring a landscape company.

3 Let your perennials grow about three years before you split them. Once you do, you've instantly saved money!

Zinnia

1

annuals from seed

Get more bang for your buck by starting annuals from seed.

By Ann Wilson

Growing your own plants from seed can really translate into big-time savings.
The cost of a single seed packet that holds many potential plants is quite small
compared with prices you'd pay for multiple purchased plants. With the money you save,
you can buy those new must-have plants on your list. Plus, growing from seed helps
extend your options for planting—and offers plenty of "I did it myself" satisfaction.
Here's a look at 10 flowering annuals that are simple to start from seed.

Sunflower

2

Cleome

3

Snapdragon

4

Giant larkspur

5

Cosmos

6

Morning glory

7

Moss rose

8

French marigold

9

Dahlberg daisy

10

1. Zinnia
(Zinnia species)

Generations of gardeners have cultivated zinnias for their cheerful colors, heat tolerance and ease of care. Common zinnias (*Zinnia elegans*) come in many sizes and colors and produce flowers that can be as large as 5 inches in diameter. Creeping zinnia (*Zinnia angustifolia* or *Zinnia linearis*) plants grow to 12 inches high and 18 inches wide and bear daisylike orange blossoms. Mexican zinnias (*Zinnia haageneana*) generally feature bicolored flowers in shades of brown, russet, deep yellow, burgundy, red or maroon.

2. Sunflower
(Helianthus annuus)

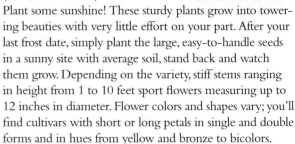

Plant some sunshine! These sturdy plants grow into towering beauties with very little effort on your part. After your last frost date, simply plant the large, easy-to-handle seeds in a sunny site with average soil, stand back and watch them grow. Depending on the variety, stiff stems ranging in height from 1 to 10 feet sport flowers measuring up to 12 inches in diameter. Flower colors and shapes vary; you'll find cultivars with short or long petals in single and double forms and in hues from yellow and bronze to bicolors.

5. Giant larkspur
(Consolida ajacis)

A spectacular substitute for the perennial delphinium, larkspur is a must for cottage gardens. A cool-weather annual, larkspur flowers from spring into midsummer and reblooms as autumn approaches. Generally, plants produce blue to purple flowers, but hybrid cultivars are available in pink, red, white and salmon. Plants grow to 3 feet high and 18 inches wide and prefer sunny sites but benefit from afternoon shade in the South. In the North, direct-sow seeds as soon as soil can be worked. Southern gardeners may want to sow seed in fall so plants develop strong roots over the winter.

6. Cosmos
(Cosmos bipinnatus)

Cosmos are a favorite for their pink, red or white flowers with bright yellow centers. The easily maintained and freely flowering plants grow to 4 feet high and 2 feet wide and may naturalize when conditions are right. Hybrid cultivars boast single, semidouble or double flowers in a wide array of sizes and hues, including bicolored varieties. The warm-weather annual prefers sunny sites and well-drained average soil. Direct-sow seed into gardens after the danger of frost has passed, or start seeds indoors six to eight weeks before your area's last frost date.

8. Moss rose
(Portulaca grandiflora)

This highly adaptable annual thrives where many annuals won't grow. Ideally suited to grow in hot, sunny spots with poor soil, these drought-tolerant succulents produce single, semidouble or double flowers in shades of red, rose, orange, yellow and white. Reddish stems and fleshy green leaves sprawl into ground-hugging mats that rarely reach more than 8 inches in height. Direct-sow seed into gardens after the danger of frost has passed, or start seeds indoors six to eight weeks before your last frost date.

9. French marigold
(Tagetes patula)

This drought-tolerant half-hardy annual is valued for its abundant single or double gold, yellow, maroon, mahogany and bicolored blooms that bloom from May into autumn—sometimes weathering a few light frosts before the end of the season. The plants grow to 12 inches high and 18 inches wide and prefer sunny sites and moist, well-draining soil but will tolerate light shade and dry soil. Direct-sow seed into gardens after the danger of frost has passed, or start seeds indoors six to eight weeks before your last frost date.

3
Cleome
(*Cleome hassleriana*)

Commonly called spider flower for its rounded blooms with spidery stamens, cleome's flowers explode in hues of white, purple, pink or bicolors. Vigorous plants grow between 3 and 6 feet tall and up to 2 feet wide and are well suited to growing at the back of borders or in the center of circular beds. Though it prefers sites with average soil and lots of sun, cleome tolerates partial shade. Direct-sow into gardens after the danger of frost has passed, or start seeds indoors six to eight weeks before your area's last frost date.

4
Snapdragon
(*Antirrhinum majus*)

Snapdragons bear tubular flowers that sprout along stems growing between 6 inches and 3 feet tall. Dwarf, intermediate and tall cultivars produce lavender, orange, pink, red, yellow or white blooms from spring through early summer. The cool-season plants prefer sunny sites with moist, organic-rich, well-draining soil. Though seeds can be directly sown in the garden, snapdragons, which grow best in cool conditions, are best started indoors six to eight weeks before your last frost date.

7
Morning glory
(*Ipomea purpurea*)

These twining vines quickly scale trellises and fences before bursting with trumpet-shaped blossoms that open with the sun and close as daylight fades. The species boasts white-throated purple flowers, but hybrid cultivars are available with white, blue, pink and magenta blooms. Morning glories prefer full sun and average soil. Direct-sow seed into gardens after the danger of frost has passed, or start seeds indoors six to eight weeks before your last frost date. For optimal germination, soak seeds overnight in water and use a knife to notch each one before planting.

10
Dahlberg daisy
(*Thymophylla tenuiloba*)

Blanketflower

Also known as golden fleece, this cold-tender perennial produces prolific yellow daisy-shaped flowers across fragrant, spreading plants 10 to 12 inches tall. Although seeds can be directly sown in the garden after last frost, it will take four months for seeded plants to bloom—so this is an annual you may want to start indoors in flats eight to 10 weeks before your area's last frost date. Plant transplants (or sow seeds where the growing season is long) in full sun and sandy to average quick-draining soil after danger of frost has passed.

Big Color on a Budget

These nine easy-care plants are guaranteed to please with colorful blooms at low-cost prices.

Canna	Blanketflower
Celosia	Lily
Croton	Butterfly bush
Ornamental sage	Catmint
	Rose

DIANA AUBUCHON

Photo How-To

We're proud to have some of the best reader and professional nature photographers around. Enjoy these amazing images, and learn a few photo tips and tricks along the way.

1,000 Birds **70**

Take Photos Like a Pro **74**

Double Exposure **80**

Starting Young **82**

Fabulous Flower Photos **84**

Photos of the Year **86**

This photographer has a long journey in front of him.

1,000 BIRDS

Chapter 3

Harlequin duck

Story and photos by Nick Kontonicolas
Egg Harbor Township, New Jersey

My grandfather is the one who taught me about the thrill of the hunt. I was born in a remote village in northwest Greece, and when I was about 10, he let me join him on his daylong hunting trips.

Many years later, when he was in his late 70s, my grandfather crossed the Atlantic to stay with my family in south Jersey. He spent most of his time watching nature shows on TV, so in an attempt to get him outside, I started taking him to the local wildlife refuge.

Those visits rekindled my love of observing nature and birds. And I soon realized that I had some of my grandfather's hunting instincts. I never did like

Ivory gull

Lapland longspur

Bald eagle

tales from the road

Nov. 29, 2009
Cape May, New Jersey
On Jan. 18, 2009, I first heard reports of an ivory gull sighting in Gloucester, Massachusetts. I drove more than six hours one Saturday to try to spot the flier for myself, but the trip was a dud. While I was there, though, I bumped into a few other birders. One had driven 11 hours straight and another had grabbed a plane from Texas, so I guess I didn't have much reason to complain. The fall of that same year, I heard about another ivory gull sighting about 35 miles from my house. I got there as fast as I could and got several pics of this beautiful bird.

Dec. 21, 2003
Barnegat Light, New Jersey
After spending the morning taking pictures of harlequin ducks, I was headed to my car when I noticed some Lapland longspurs feeding in the nearby dunes. I got down and started inching toward them. Suddenly, my camera started flashing its low-battery light, so no more pictures for me. But that little bird walked right toward me, getting about six feet away. When I finally got up to leave, the longspur didn't seem to notice me at all!

Feb. 9, 2006
Skagit Flats, Washington
During a trip to northwest Washington, I saw many bald eagles. This adult seemed to be having a standoff with its reflection before it finally decided to go ahead and have a drink.

You can follow Nick's progress on his website, 1000birds.com.

the killing part, though, so I decided to go hunting with my camera.

Pretty soon, I set a goal to keep me motivated. I decided I would take photos of 1,000 different bird species. This is about 10 percent of all the bird species in the world, which seemed like a realistic and challenging goal.

I'm currently at around 550. I can probably get another 100 to 150 North American species, and then the rest will have to come from trips to South America, Asia or Africa.

Unfortunately, I'm the only one in my family interested in birding. So it's not always easy to lure my wife and two daughters, one in high school and the other in college, on outings with me when we travel.

We find ways to make it work, though. For instance, we've been to Costa Rica twice. While my family stays at the resort, I go running around the forest to chase birds instead. And we had a similar situation on a vacation to Punta Cana in the Dominican Republic. (I'm always looking for resorts near forests!)

I've been at this for nearly eight years. It's probably going to take me another 12 years or so to reach my goal, but I'm not in a hurry. After all, it's the thrill of the hunt that I enjoy most.

Brant ducks

Nick's favorites

ALL-TIME FAVORITE: Ivory gulls. I spend many hours trying to capture these fliers on camera.

MOST BEAUTIFUL: Harlequin ducks.

MOST INTERESTING: Peregrine falcons. They have amazing speed and perform incredible acrobatics.

FAVORITE EXOTIC FLIER: Keel-billed toucans.

FUNNIEST: Savannah sparrows. I had one land on my head a number of times while I was in my photo blind.

MOST INTRIGUING NESTING BEHAVIOR: Least terns. They defend their nests fearlessly!

Lesser yellowlegs

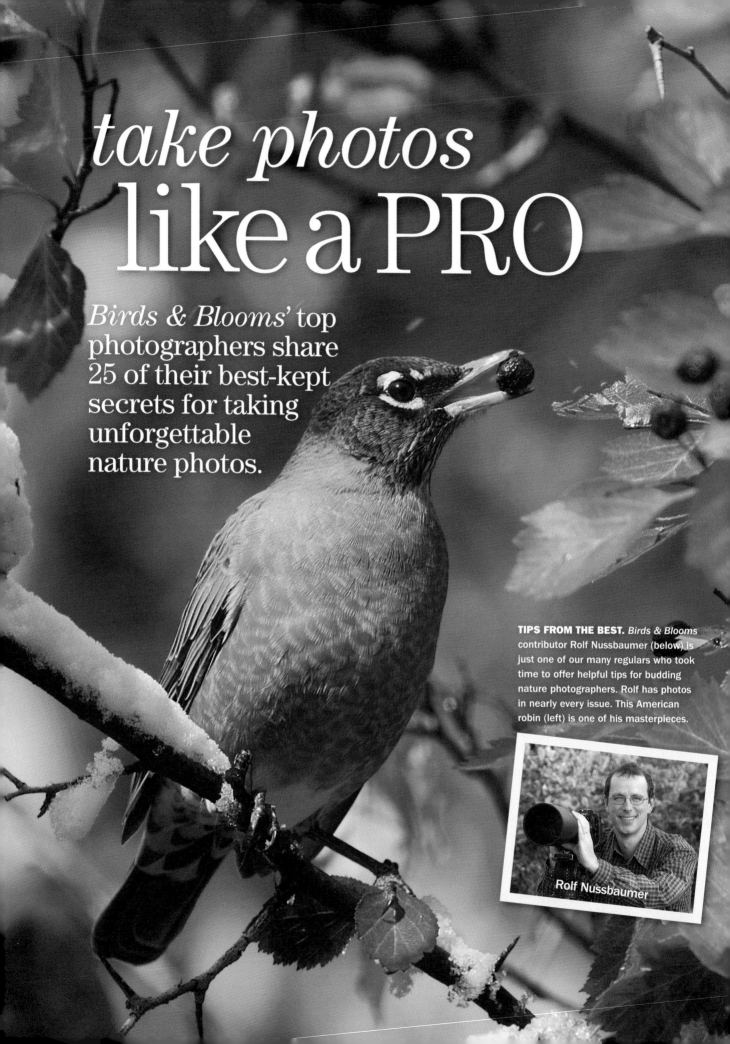

take photos like a PRO

Birds & Blooms' top photographers share 25 of their best-kept secrets for taking unforgettable nature photos.

TIPS FROM THE BEST. *Birds & Blooms* contributor Rolf Nussbaumer (below) is just one of our many regulars who took time to offer helpful tips for budding nature photographers. Rolf has photos in nearly every issue. This American robin (left) is one of his masterpieces.

Rolf Nussbaumer

Here at *Birds & Blooms*, we take special pride in our photography. We carefully select and scrutinize each photo to make sure it's the best of its kind. Of course, we wouldn't be anywhere without our talented group of photographers. They are the best in the business and really make the magazine come alive.

We recently asked a few of them to share some of their favorite stories from the field and picture-taking tips with you. Wow, were we delighted with what they had to offer! Whether you're a seasoned photographer or a budding hobbyist, you're sure to learn a lot.

Creative Compositions

1 A basic photo technique that can immediately improve your picture is to consider the point of view. In most cases, it's preferable to try to get at eye level with the subject. This results in better eye contact and a greater sense of intimacy.

—DAVE MASLOWSKI

2 Place important elements off center to keep the image from becoming static. Look for leading lines, or shoot on an angle to add a sense of movement. —LINDA DETRICK

3 Experiment with different angles until you find the subject's best side. Some images are best when most of the surroundings are shown, while others are more successful up close.

—ROLF NUSSBAUMER

4 When composing a photo, look for something that sets the image apart. It can be as simple as a nodding bud, a curled fern frond or a single leaf.

—LINDA DETRICK

Dave Maslowski

Setting the Scene

The belted kingfisher is known to perch on the same spot time and time again, but this species also tends to be wary of people and difficult to photograph.

Attempting to get a memorable shot, I found a piece of driftwood on the shore of a river and propped it up by the water. I returned the next afternoon, hoping the kingfishers had become accustomed to their new spot, only to find that their perch was gone. I hastily found another piece of driftwood and set it up in the same spot. I was waiting behind my makeshift blind when a female landed on the driftwood (left) and I took some photos. Sometimes you need to set the stage to catch the elusive species. —DAVE MASLOWSKI

Nature's Second Chances

Where I live in Texas, the bluebonnets bloom every spring in March (above). When you have events like this that occur the same time and place every year, you can start to plan your shots. If I don't catch the photo I want, I get a second chance the following year. I remind myself of this when scarlet tanagers, northern parula and other warblers fly from the tropics to Texas every spring, or when the snow geese come by the thousands to spend winter on our prairies.

—KATHY ADAMS CLARK

Kathy Adams Clark

Carol L. Edwards

5 Move in closer to your subject, cropping out anything that isn't important to your picture. You can walk closer or use your zoom. The idea is to fill the frame, whether you're photographing your best friend or a prize dahlia in the garden. —MARK TURNER

6 Try to avoid a messy background unless it adds to your image. Otherwise, it can be very distracting. —ROLF NUSSBAUMER

7 Many birds look their best on lightly overcast days because you'll get incredible feather detail and vivid colors. Don't include water in the frame on those days, though, because gray water is unattractive in most pictures. —MARIE READ

Elusive Owl

A fellow birder shared news that a northern hawk owl was seen on a nearby ski trail. I really wanted to photograph this owl, so a friend and I trekked out in a small red sleigh, hoping not to sink down in the deep snow. We spent hours searching and were about to give up when I saw a dark shape fly through the trees and perch in an opening. We watched in awe as it preened. It was an experience I'll never forget, and I have the photos to prove it! —CAROL L. EDWARDS

Technical Tips Made Easy

8 Learn how to use shutter speed to your advantage. It takes a shutter speed of 1/60th of a second to stop a living creature that is standing still. It takes 1/250th of a second to stop something that's walking or a flower moving in the breeze. The faster the speed, the more movement is stopped. —KATHY ADAMS CLARK

9 To get a blurred background effect, you need to use a lower aperture setting, usually f5.6 or less. To get the opposite effect for more depth of field, use a higher aperture, f16 or f22. If these settings sound foreign to you, it's time to get your camera manual and read up a bit. —ROLF NUSSBAUMER

10 Tripods can be cumbersome in flower beds, so I use a monopod instead. Monopods are mobile and allow you to get closer to butterflies. Plus, they keep me from damaging surrounding flowers in my wife Susan's garden. —RICHARD DAY

11 The histogram is the graph on the back of your camera. You see it after you've taken the photo on a digital SLR camera. Some smaller cameras show the histogram while you're composing the photo. Learn how to read the histogram for better images. For example, if you see a spike on the right side, you've overexposed the white areas of the photo. —KATHY ADAMS CLARK

12 Set your camera for its highest-quality mode, capturing the most information it is capable of in the biggest file. You can always make a smaller copy to e-mail to a friend later, but resolution (number of pixels) and quality (look for words like "superfine" or "fine" or an icon with smooth edges) are most important. This might mean you'll need more memory cards, but they're small and light and have become quite cheap! —MARK TURNER

13 The best light is in the first two hours of the morning and the last two of the evening. But if you're forced to shoot in the harsh light of the day or on a heavy overcast day, simply use a fill flash. Set your flash at a setting of –1 to –2 stops. This will help remove shadows on your subject. —ROLF NUSSBAUMER

Sap-sicle for a Chickadee

A late-winter ice storm broke a branch off a birch tree next to my house, and overnight the rising sap dripped out and froze to form an icicle.

The chickadees discovered the icicle, and as it began melting they would hover to sip from it. I wanted to capture this on film, so I aimed my camera at the tip of the icicle and waited. Finally, this chickadee seemed to pose for me, and I captured this image—one of my all-time favorites. —MARIE READ

Marie Read

Mark Turner

Penstemon on a Precipice

While hiking the slopes of Mount Baker, the 10,778-foot snow-capped volcano near my home in Washington, I meandered to the edge of the dramatic Deming Glacier.

I don't recommend crossing a glacier alone without an ice ax, but I'd been on the glacier before and felt confident I could avoid crevasses by picking my route carefully.

I found this spot filled with clumps of Davidson's penstemon growing right at the edge of the precipice. I had only my pocket digital camera (I didn't want to carry all my equipment on this path!), but I was able to take advantage of the afternoon backlighting and dramatic clouds forming over the mountains. The hike was worth it when I saw the results.

—MARK TURNER

14 For action shots, ditch your tripod. I'm usually an advocate of tripods, but if the action is fast and furious, hand holding gives you better mobility. Be sure to use a fast shutter speed so your photos are sharp.

—MARIE READ

Be Prepared!

15 Keep on the lookout for birds doing something interesting for your photos: feeding young, eating berries or bathing, for instance.

—RICHARD DAY

16 The best bird photographers are also bird-watchers. They're observant and understand bird behavior. When you're not photograph-ing, watch the birds closely to learn about their lives. This will help you pick up on the subtle cues they give when they're about to do something interesting, dramatic and photogenic.

—MARIE READ

17 Don't forget the importance of having flowering and fruiting plants in your backyard or at a nearby park. They are wonderful animal magnets and make great photo areas. Spend time watching these plants to see what comes. Just this summer I counted more than eight caterpillars, three spiders, five butterflies and a hummingbird in less than 10 minutes in a small patch of blooming plants. —ROLF NUSSBAUMER

18 Create vignettes of garden art and flowers in your own backyard where birds will land to complete the picture. When situating them, keep in mind where the light will fall at different times of day.

—CAROL L. EDWARDS

19 Like me, some birds have a favorite "easy chair" or a particular spot they frequent. Learn where it is and start planning your shots accordingly. —DAVE MASLOWSKI

Richard Day

Duck Tales

For weeks, I tried to photograph the baby wood ducks that fledged from one of our nest boxes. But the mother kept her young hidden in the grasses out of my camera's range. I was about ready to give up altogether when I saw the mom swim out and preen on a log in front of my blind. Then, one by one, the four ducklings popped up beside her, giving me the opportunity to take several pictures. It wasn't until I was editing the film later that I discovered this photo (above). It looks as if the mama is scolding her kids. It's one of my favorite photos, and it proves that patience and persistence really can pay off! —RICHARD DAY

Keep It Fun

20 Take a picture of your garden every Saturday to document how your flowers change through the season. Then share a digital scrapbook with friends and family. Seeing how plants grew—or didn't—each year will also help you plan your garden for next year. —SUSAN DAY

21 Don't be afraid to make mistakes. Who hasn't looked at a picture and thought, *What was I thinking?* It's impossible to know exactly how every detail will turn out in the final picture. I like to remind myself: If you're not making mistakes, you're not trying hard enough. —DAVE MASLOWSKI

22 When you're photographing out in nature, it's always best to anticipate action. I once captured great photos of an egret because I knew where it was roosting. At the end of the day, I was ready with my tripod and camera. —ROLAND JORDAHL

23 It's not easy to see birds while zipping along highways, so consider a leisurely back-roads drive to slow down and see what is sitting on that fence post or bit of rusty wire. —CAROL L. EDWARDS

24 Explore the outskirts. Parks are usually well-groomed, but head over to where the weedy areas start. You might find an American goldfinch enjoying some thistles or a red-winged blackbird calling from a marsh reed. —CAROL L. EDWARDS

25 Don't give up on your shot. For instance, if you're trying to capture a butterfly or dragonfly at a particular plant and it flies away, just stand still and wait. Chances are it will be back, and you'll be ready to get your shot. —ROLAND JORDAHL

Double exposure

Husband and wife make photography a team effort.

Story by Suzette Brumbaugh, York, Pennsylvania   Photos by Suzette and Blair Brumbaugh

I began taking pictures at age 8, when my father gave me my first box camera. But as an adult, I didn't feel that my photos captured the true beauty of the landscape. I always wondered how the pros got such beautiful nature shots. So my husband and I took a photo workshop. That's when the bug really bit us!

We continued to learn together by attending workshops, reading books and studying accomplished photographers. We've had many cameras over the years. Today, Blair still prefers his film camera, while I use digital.

Since retiring a few years ago, we've been happily roaming the country by RV in search of striking landscapes and other subjects. Public gardens, wildlife refuges, and state and national parks give us the opportunity for distinctive nature shots.

When we're not on the road, we're at home gardening and maintaining a backyard oasis for birds and other creatures. We can spend hours snapping flowers, birds, insects and wildlife.

Our goal is to keep improving our skills. And along the way, we hope to share with others a little bit of what we've learned.

Azalea

Star Gazer lily

Photo tips from Suzette and Blair

Slow down. We always look the area over for the best angle before we even get our cameras out. Sometimes it takes an hour before we snap our first picture.

Always use a tripod. You'll be surprised how much sharper your pictures turn out.

Try different angles. You can really improve an image just by changing the angle, and by trying the same shot as a horizontal and as a vertical.

Keep it simple. We believe that less is more. Don't overdo it with composition.

Go back to your favorites. Everyone has favorite spots. Visit them often to check out the mood of every season and the light at different times of day.

Back to basics. Go online or find a book and read up on the basic rules of composition. Checking the edges of your frame, not centering all your photographs and other simple guidelines are always helpful.

Watch the background. By moving a foot or two to either side, you can avoid distracting elements and light spots in the background.

Timing is everything. Shoot in soft morning or golden evening light.

Brown pelican

Trillium

"We can spend hours *snapping flowers, birds, insects and wildlife."*

Red-shouldered hawk

Snowy egret

Starting young

Learn a few secrets from a budding bird photographer.

Story and photos by Connor Yamane, Lake Park, Minnesota

When I was 4 years old, Grandpa Rod started teaching me about birds. My grandparents live in a cabin on a lake—an ideal spot to watch birds year-round.

Grandpa gave me my first camera when I was 9 and started teaching me how to take pictures. I'm now almost 11, and we have identified more than 100 species of birds together. I've photographed quite a few of these birds with my Canon XTI and have been able to get amazing pictures.

To get the perfect spot to photograph birds, Grandpa and I set up a feeding area in the trees near the shore. We also walk around the lake and ponds on our country road. There are several birding sanctuaries close to home that we visit: Maplewood State Park, Itasca State Park and Tamarac National Wildlife Refuge.

Rose-breasted grosbeak

One of my favorite ways to observe and photograph the birds is to go kayaking to the lake's three islands. I also kayak the local rivers with my dad and grandpa. On one kayak outing on the lake, we spotted more than 15 different species of birds, and a doe with two fawns jumping over a creek.

Between the bird encounters, my grandpa is teaching me to study my surroundings and to photograph things such as flowers, insects and amphibians. I even won first place in a local photography contest for my dragonfly photo.

By studying many bird books and observing birds in their natural environment, I've learned a lot about birds and their behavior. It is really fun to see a species for the first time, and it is very exciting to get a picture to share with others.

My favorite year-round birds to photograph are woodpeckers. A pair of pileated woodpeckers visit the lakeshore near me. It is fun to watch them and take pictures.

What's next? Maybe I'll be an ornithologist someday. But one thing is certain: I plan to continue my birding and photographic pursuits indefinitely, thanks to my grandpa.

Ruby-throated hummingbird

Photo tips from Connor

1. Study the birds' habits and observe them as much as possible in their natural environment.
2. Move slowly and stay quiet. By sitting or standing still, you will become part of the surroundings, and quite often the birds will come close to you.
3. Imagine what you want in your mind's eye before you click the shutter button. Then try to frame the shot with the best position of the bird, the background and the angle.
4. To get as sharp an image as possible, focus on the bird's eye.
5. Practice patience, patience and more patience!

Bald eagle

"My favorite year-round birds to photograph are *woodpeckers*."

Red-bellied woodpecker

Common loon

Dragonfly

Fabulous flower *photos*

A passion for taking pictures inspired her to expand her garden. By Diana Aubuchon, Overland Park, Kansas

Anemone

Since I was born on what is now called Earth Day, it's only fitting that I enjoy being outdoors, admiring and photographing nature's greatest subjects.

I received my first camera for my ninth birthday and immediately proceeded to take pictures of everything in sight. I'm sure my parents wondered what they'd gotten themselves into when they saw the charges for film processing!

But it wasn't until I moved into my own home that I really became serious about photographing flowers. I love gardening, and I had more time to concentrate on growing flowers and photographing them. I quickly learned that the more experience I had, the better the photos became. Thank goodness for digital photography and no more film processing charges.

I grow more than 100 varieties of daylilies. I also have a number of Oriental lilies—my favorite is the red-colored Star Gazer lily. Last year I began growing irises. I had no idea they were available in so many different sizes, colors and varieties.

Of course, no garden is complete without butterflies and birds. I have planted butterfly weed, zinnias and butterfly bushes to attract butterflies. Birds are attracted to my thistle seed, sunflowers and hummingbird feeders.

My love for photography has ignited my passion for gardening. I've purposely filled my garden with an eclectic collection of plants that provide a wonderful photographic playground for me.

Daylily

Zebra swallowtail on butterfly bush

Six tips for better flower photos

1. Take pictures early in the morning while the light is soft and before the sun can damage the petals. Don't hesitate to shoot on cloudy days.

2. Use varying angles to get the best point of view. Don't be afraid to shoot the flower from below, beside or behind.

3. Look for the best color combinations. Colors at opposite sides of the color wheel always make great combinations.

4. Use a wide aperture to put the focus on the flower and blur the background.

5. Move in close and use the macro setting on your point-and-shoot camera or a macro lens on your SLR. You'll be amazed at what you see when you get close!

6. Consider buying a polarizing filter to decrease glare in water gardens or a lens hood to prevent lens flare.

Black swallowtail on
butterfly bush

"*No garden is complete without*
butterflies and birds."

Pink striped daisy

Monarch caterpillar
on butterfly weed

Backyard Photo Contest winner
Photo by Turner Coulson

Waterlilies
Photo by Dawn Currie

Black-and-white warbler
Photo by Greg Lasley / KAC Productions

Morning glory, Backyard Photo Contest finalist
Photo by Koreen Appleby

American goldfinch
Photo by Carol L. Edwards

BUD HENSLEY

CHAPTER 4

Magnificent
Hummingbirds

We know you love them!
Hummingbirds are always a reader
favorite, so we took our best tips,
photos and stories and pulled them
all together in this single chapter.

Hummingbird All-Stars **90**

Hummingbird Feeder for Pennies **94**

Gardener on a Mission **96**

Top 10: Seeing Red **102**

Containers: Red Carpet Treatment **106**

Seven Giving Gardeners **108**

Hummer Happenings **111**

Did You Know? **115**

Photos of the Year **116**

hummingbird

"Fancy Flier"

all-stars

These eight fliers are the most common hummingbirds in North America. Here's a glimpse at why they captivate so many bird-watchers across the continent.

By Anne Schmauss

COSTA'S

You can find the Costa's hummingbird most often in the very dry country of the West, generally in the deserts of Southern California and Arizona. Typically this hummer builds its tiny nest in the desert yucca plant, using materials such as bark and flowers. It binds the nest together with spider webbing and lines it with plant down. The purple gorget (throat) and crown of this hummer gives it a distinctive look.

"Desert Beauty"

ALLEN'S

You can see this flier regularly only along a strip of the California and southern Oregon coasts, where it nests. One of the earliest migrants, the Allen's hummingbird migrates north from Mexico as early as December, arriving at nesting grounds in January. Once the female lays the second clutch of eggs, the adult male wastes no time heading back to Mexico, sometimes flying south as early as mid-May. The rest of the family follows later.

"The Early Bird"

BROAD-TAILED

This hummer is often heard before it's seen, especially in spring. In flight, the male's wings make a loud, shrill buzz, letting him advertise his presence simply by flying around. Air rushing through tapered wing feathers causes this distinctive trill. As the summer goes on, these feathers become worn; by late fall, the sound made by the flying adult male is much softer.

ANNA'S

The Anna's is a common year-round resident of the West Coast. Fifty years ago, this hummingbird spent the whole year in northern Mexico, but widespread planting of exotic flowering plants in California led many of these birds to move north. The male Anna's will dive aggressively at other birds and people.

"Hometown Darling"

RUBY-THROATED

The ruby-throated hummingbird is by far the most common hummingbird in the Eastern United States and the only one that nests east of the Mississippi. The ruby-throat winters in Mexico and Central America and heads north in early spring, flying 500 miles across the Gulf of Mexico. This journey takes 18 to 22 hours! Some people have even spotted these fliers stopping on oil rigs to take a rest during their long flight.

BLACK-CHINNED

During the summer, you can find the black-chinned hummingbird throughout much of the Western United States. One of the most widespread and adaptable hummingbirds, the black-chinned is found in and around deserts, forests, mountains and urban areas. Because these hummers dart about expertly hunting for flying insects, they are tough to follow in flight. Watch for them at the ends of bare branches, where they often perch.

"Mighty Mite"

CALLIOPE

At only 3¼ inches long, the calliope hummingbird is the smallest bird in North America north of Mexico. During its courtship ritual, the male calliope flies as high as 130 feet in the air before plummeting back down to earth—and then flying back up again, making a U shape. This display is usually just one step in an exhausting effort to win over a female.

"Urban Charmer"

"Most Popular"

"Feisty Flier"

RUFOUS

Sometimes described as a bully, the rufous hummingbird is serious about defending its territory. If you live in the West, this is the hummingbird that chases away all the other birds from your feeder. The rufous nests farther north than any other hummingbird, as far as Alaska. This makes its trip back to Mexico almost 4,000 miles, among the longest migrations made by any bird in the world.

hummingbird feeder
for pennies

Window feeder doubles as a hand-held hummingbird magnet.

By Lisa Szczygiel-Durante, Thomaston, Connecticut

What You Will Need

- 12 inches of 18-gauge copper wire
- ½-inch suction cup with a hole in the base
- Plastic test tube with cap
- Decorative beads (optional)
- Artificial flower without stem
- Small wire cutters
- Pliers (for twisting and spiraling wire)

Step by step

1. This is a simple window feeder (right) that anyone can make. To start, cut an 8-inch piece from the copper wire. Let the wire naturally take a half-moon shape.

2. Lace 2 inches of the wire through the hole in the suction cup and then fold and twist the wire until secure.

3. Bend the longer end of the wire gently with your hands into an arc, leaving ¾ inch at the very end for the hook that will attach to the feeder.

4. Take your pliers and make a large loop at the very end of the arc, forming a shepherd's hook, with the open end on the top or facing up. This will make it easier to attach the feeding tube quickly and will prevent the feeder from falling off.

5. Take the remaining 4 inches of copper wire and wrap it around the

test tube, with one end much longer than the other. Use pliers to twist and secure the wire to the test tube. This should leave a ¾-inch tail remaining to attach a decorative glass bead.

6. Slide the ring you have made more than halfway up the tube, so that when full, the feeder will stay up.

7. Slide another bead onto the open end of the wire wrapped around the tube and use pliers to spiral the wire and close it up completely. Now the copper wire is wrapped firmly around the feeding tube and you have a loop to attach to your hook with the suction cup.

8. Make a small hole in the tube's cap, place it on the tube and poke the end of the artificial flower through the center so that the hummingbirds can get at the nectar as naturally as

Hand-Feeding Basics

Lisa has perfected the art of feeding hummingbirds by hand. She has developed the Hum-Fi hand-held feeder, pictured at left (*hum-fi.com*), and offers these tips to beginners.

Ready? Put the feeder where you can easily see it from indoors.

Set. Let the window do the work. Give the hummers time to get comfortable feeding from this feeder first.

Go! Once the birds fly away, hold the feeder in your hand facing away from you. Stay as still as possible. Once the birds get used to you, they'll approach you without fear!

possible. If the flower doesn't have a hole in it, make one with a pin.

9. Attach the closed loop on the tube to the upward-facing shepherd's hook with the suction cup. Make sure your window is clean so the suction cup will be secure.

10. Voilà! You now have a nifty little hummingbird feeder of your own. Place it in a window where you can easily view it!

The best thing about this feeder is that it also works great for hand-feeding. —LISA

gardener on a mission

The plan is simple:
Grow a great garden.
Attract hummingbirds.
Take fabulous photos.

Photos and story by Bud Hensley
Middleton, Ohio

WHEN I WAS A KID, gardening was always something my mom enjoyed. I never really understood her fascination with dirt, shovels and plants, but I knew that hanging around with her was the perfect way to find night crawlers, pill bugs and all sorts of other tiny critters.

I've always loved photography and nature but never really combined the two interests until spring 2004. My girlfriend, Michele, and I made a decision that would change our springs and summers forever: We dug up half our yard for a hummingbird and butterfly garden.

Six years later, we're officially obsessed. What started as a small garden with a few coneflowers, bee balms and butterfly bushes now boasts dozens of native perennials and nectar-rich annuals.

Our first summer was exciting, and we felt fortunate to see two hummingbirds at one time in our yard. Every year since, our traffic has increased. It's so rewarding to watch these fliers flitting around the yard from bloom to bloom.

When it comes to taking pictures of hummingbirds, I've learned that it's not

Female ruby-throat
at wild dagga

Female ruby-throat
at salvia

Ruby-throat
at bee balm

Juvenile ruby-throat
at Chilean glory vine

While Bud uses lots of red
blooms in his yard, he says it's
not the only solution. Every yard
is different, he says. Find out
what the hummingbirds in your
area like most, and then expand
from there.

Female ruby-throat
at cardinal flower

Juvenile ruby-throat

just about being good with your hoe or your camera. The two go hand in hand. Here are my tips for creating a hummingbird-friendly backyard and capturing stunning shots at the same time.

Know your camera. There are a variety of cameras on the market today that will allow you to get excellent images of hummingbirds. But what's most important is that you take the time to understand your equipment's capabilities, as well as its limitations.

Find support. Tripods are great, but the fast and elusive nature of a hummingbird's flight makes it hard to use one. Instead, I always carry a small towel or beanbag and use it to support my camera. The crook of a tree, windowsill or deck railing can do the job, too. Find a solid surface that works for you.

Create the right environment. First of all, you want to make sure you have enough perches for hummingbirds to land, preen and rest. If you don't have many natural perches, make more with dead branches. Next, try to establish your hummingbird area so that the sun is to your back when you observe them. This will allow you to capture greater detail in the feathers.

Female ruby-throat at
David Verity cigar plant

Bud's 5 favorite
hummingbird plants

1. Bee balm. The Jacob Cline cultivar has clusters of bright-red tubes of nectar from May until August (with deadheading). It's a showy perennial that's easy to grow, and this cultivar resists mildew.

2. Trumpet honeysuckle. It's available in red, orange and yellow blooms with names such as Alabama Crimson, Blanche Sandman and Major Wheeler. This vine blooms the entire season.

3. Salvia. There are too many to list and we love them all. Lady in Red is one of our favorite annuals because it's easy to grow from seed.

4. Cigar plant. This annual blooms all summer and grows rapidly. The plant is very easy to propagate from cuttings, which you can overwinter indoors.

5. Cardinal flower. This Midwest native perennial blooms from August until the end of October, coinciding with the ruby-throated hummingbird's fall migration.

Female ruby-throat at royal catchfly

Plant the right blooms. Learn which plants grow in your area, and plant a garden that blooms from spring through fall with nectar-rich flowers.

Be patient. When photographing a hummingbird, pay attention to its behavior. After a while, you can often anticipate where it will go next. It takes time to earn their trust so they will come around when you're outside. Position yourself close to the blooms that get the most visits, and then wait for the hummingbirds to come to you. Wait until they get used to you before you bring out your camera and start snapping away.

I love photographing hummingbirds because they fascinate me. There's no other creature on the planet like them, with their tremendous speed, precise aerial maneuvering, fierce determination and incredible iridescent glimmer, all on that diminutive feathered frame.

They are truly a wonder of nature. Setting out to capture all that attitude and beauty in your own backyard is both a challenge and a joy.

photographer secrets

Try a few of these tips from Bud for unique photo opportunities.

Water entertainment. Hummingbirds love water, especially on hot summer days. Try setting a sprinkler or mister near a perching spot. It won't take long for them to find it and provide some outstanding entertainment! Just make sure you protect your camera from the moisture.

Fruit fly bliss. Try placing some rotting fruit in a small container to attract fruit flies. Insects can be a large portion of an immature hummingbird's diet, and it's intriguing to watch one probe a piece of fruit in search of tiny bugs.

Hover perfection. Using an inexpensive single-port feeder, you can easily capture a hummingbird hovering in midair. Bud suggests limiting the number of feeders available when attempting this. Position yourself so that the hummingbird is in the same plane of view when it backs away as it is drinking. Snap the shot with a high shutter speed. It may take a few attempts to get the timing down, but you'll master it with practice.

Perfect perches. Some of Bud's favorite wildlife images are of hummingbirds stretching and preening. "They are amazing little contortionists and it's difficult to fully appreciate the range of their flexibility until you take the time to observe one going through its routine," he says. "If your camera allows you to adjust the shutter speed, set it for 1/500th of a second or faster. Hummingbirds move fast, even when they're resting."

Ruby-throat at trumpet vine flower

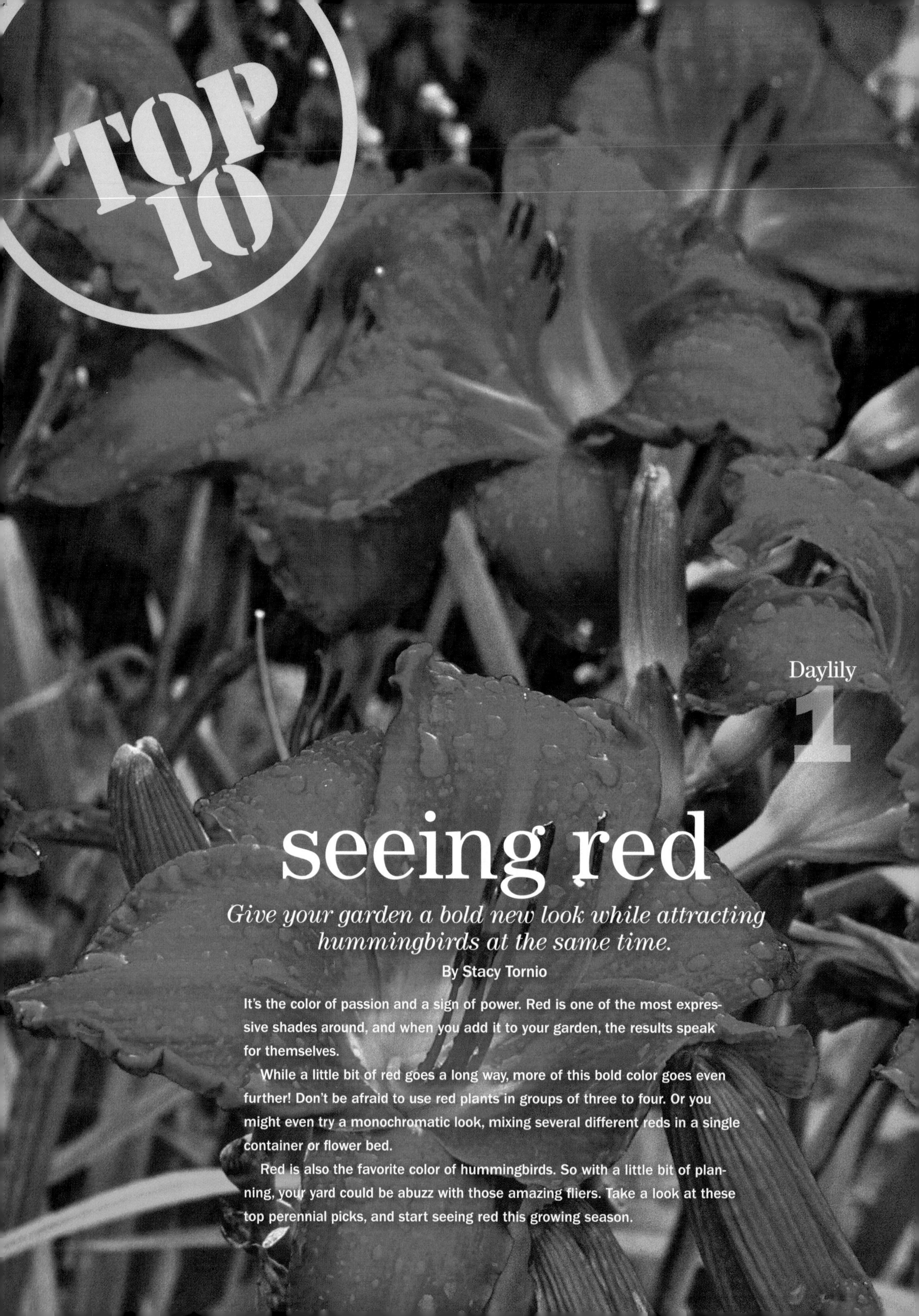

Daylily

1

seeing red

Give your garden a bold new look while attracting hummingbirds at the same time.

By Stacy Tornio

It's the color of passion and a sign of power. Red is one of the most expressive shades around, and when you add it to your garden, the results speak for themselves.

While a little bit of red goes a long way, more of this bold color goes even further! Don't be afraid to use red plants in groups of three to four. Or you might even try a monochromatic look, mixing several different reds in a single container or flower bed.

Red is also the favorite color of hummingbirds. So with a little bit of planning, your yard could be abuzz with those amazing fliers. Take a look at these top perennial picks, and start seeing red this growing season.

Columbine

2

Cardinal flower

3

Penstemon

4

Bee balm

5

Hibiscus

6

Peony

7

Coral bells

8

Garden phlox

9

Oriental poppy

10

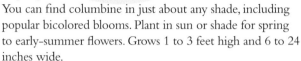

1

Daylily

(*Hemerocallis*, Zones 3 to 10)

You'll have blooms all summer when you plant this back-yard favorite. Grow just about any shade imaginable in full sun or partial shade. They reach 10 inches to 4 feet tall and 1½ to 4 feet wide.

Why we love it: It's a snap to share daylilies with friends. Divide them every three to five years to revitalize and to prevent crowding.

2

Columbine

(*Aquilegia*, Zones 3 to 9)

You can find columbine in just about any shade, including popular bicolored blooms. Plant in sun or shade for spring to early-summer flowers. Grows 1 to 3 feet high and 6 to 24 inches wide.

Why we love it: It's a wonderful companion plant. Pair red-and-white columbine with blue pansies for an easy, early patriotic display.

5

Bee balm

(*Monarda didyma*, Zones 3 to 9)

You can find newer bee balm varieties in purple, pink and white, but the classic red shade is still best at luring hummingbirds. Grows 3 to 4 feet high and up to 26 inches wide. It grows in full sun but will also tolerate afternoon shade.

Why we love it: Bumblebees, butterflies and humming-birds just can't resist it, and the unique shapes of the blooms add interest to any perennial bed.

6

Hibiscus

(*Hibiscus* species, Zones 4 to 10)

Bold, beautiful and impressive, this perennial grows up to 15 feet tall. Its huge blooms are 4 to 12 inches wide and last from early summer to the first frost. Keep this stunner in full sun and in rich, moist soil.

Why we love it: Look for tropical species of these plants to add to your favorite container display. One plant alone will add a gorgeous touch of the tropics.

9

Garden phlox

(*Phlox paniculata*, Zones 3 to 8)

Garden phlox is a resilient plant that continues blooming throughout the season with the help of a little deadheading. Grow this charmer in full sun. It reaches up to 36 inches high and wide.

Why we love it: Newer varieties resist powdery mildew. Ask your local nursery for mildew-resistant picks, or look for the Flame series.

10

Oriental poppy

(*Papaver orientale*, Zones 4 to 9)

Poppies always look better in bunches. Plant these ruby-red dazzlers in spring, sowing the very fine seeds directly into the soil. By early summer the following year, you should see the signature fuzzy buds and cup-shaped blooms. Plants grow up to 36 inches tall.

Why we love it: When the blooms are spent, the seedpods make attractive additions to wreaths or fall arrangements.

3

Cardinal flower

(*Lobelia cardinalis,* Zones 3 to 9)

There's a reason this plant was named after such a beautiful bird. The scarlet flowers light up gardens, growing up to 4 feet high and 2 feet wide. You can grow it in partial shade to full sun.

Why we love it: This beauty seems to reach out and beckon hummingbirds. Plant several in one spot, and you're sure to see a flying jewel hovering in your garden.

4

Penstemon

(*Penstemon,* Zones 3 to 9)

You can grow these cheerful, colorful trumpets in full sun to light shade. Grow in well-drained soils, and most will tolerate droughty conditions once established.

Why we love it: The blooms might look delicate, but they pack quite a punch, especially when you group several of them together.

7

Peony

(*Paeonia,* Zones 3 to 8)

Giant blooms in spring and early summer offer loads of sweetness for butterflies and hummingbirds. They grow up to 3½ feet tall and wide. Dig and divide the rhizomes in fall.

Why we love it: You can make a big impact with just one peony plant. For a spectacular shade, try the Karl Rosenfield cultivar pictured here.

8

Coral bells

(*Heuchera,* Zones 3 to 9)

Known primarily for its fabulous foliage, this tough perennial also offers distinctive bell-shaped blooms. It grows up to 3 feet high when in bloom and 24 inches wide, blooming in late spring to early summer. For red blooms, look for the cultivars Blood Red, Lipstick and Havana.

Why we love it: While it won't do well in heavy shade, coral bells will make it in partial. Go ahead and give it a try. You just might discover it to be a fabulous alternative to shade-loving hostas.

Ready for Red

They might be newer to the scene, but these perennial favorites from *perennialresource.com* show why red is a can't-miss color for any bloom.

Coneflower. This Hot Papaya echinacea (left) was introduced in 2009. It boasts spicy red-orange flowers with a pom-pom center.

Coreopsis. Cultivar Caliente has crimson blooms that go a long way: Just one plant should provide you with reliable color all summer long.

Yarrow. This drought-tough perennial most commonly comes in yellow, but now you can get red and pink hues, thanks to cultivars like Strawberry Seduction and Paprika.

containers
red carpet
treatment

Woo hummingbirds with containers full of red blooms.

Sometimes the most beautiful and effective containers hold only one type of plant. This 14-inch-diameter container filled with red cuphea will be a hit with hummingbirds.

Simply Stylish

You'll need only three Totally Tempted® cuphea plants for this container. Sun-loving, it blooms through fall and doesn't need deadheading.

Create a hummingbird haven with bright red blooms, and watch as these pretty fliers flock to your backyard.

Tropical Treat

The tropical feel of this container will attract more than hummingbirds! Grown in an 18-inch-diameter container, this trio will brighten up your backyard.

A 1 **Bourbon Street copperleaf plant**
B 2 **Burning Bush coral begonia**
C 2 **Superbells® Red calibrachoa**

Seeing Red

This simple, stunning container combination will brighten up a table or basket. Plant it in a 14-inch-diameter pot for best results.

A 2 **Superbells® Red calibrachoa**
B 2 **Dolce® Peach Melba coral bells**

seven
giving
gardeners

*Meet people across the country
who open their backyards
to hummingbird fans.*

By Ann Wilson

Hummingbirds have a mesmerizing effect on people. From large festivals to banding demonstrations, no other bird is honored by so many colorful events. The seven owners of the four gardens featured here are among the most dedicated hummingbird fans in North America, even opening up their own backyards to complete strangers who share their interest. If you happen to be in their areas, be sure to look them up!

Washington Artist Finds Inspiration From Nature

Lisa Hill, a watercolorist in Richmond, Washington, finds subjects for her paintings right outside her door. She and husband Larry Umthum have installed a 6-foot-deep hummingbird border that stretches 50 feet along the edge of a steep slope overlooking the Yakima River (pictured at right).

"Almost all my paintings are inspired by my gardens and the wildlife that visits them," Lisa says. "When we moved here four and a half years ago, we had 10 plant varieties hummingbirds love. Now we have hundreds of plant species in different areas of our yard."

Lisa's border, which blooms from May through August and beyond, is packed with hummingbird favorites. Some of her best performers include pink and peach agastache, penstemons blooming in red and pink, hot-pink monardas, red crocosmia, red-flowering salvia and cardinal flower.

Want to pay Lisa a visit? Just send her an e-mail at *lisa@lisahillwatercolorist.com*.

"Why should Larry and I be the only ones to enjoy these marvelous sights?" she says.

Humble Hummingbirder From Minnesota

Dolores Hagen's extensive gardens in Henderson, Minnesota, are located in the Minnesota River Valley flyway. Come August, her landscape draws in bevies of ruby-throated hummingbirds and thousands of visitors.

"It's funny—I'm not a real gardener, but I like flowers and I like birds," says Dolores. "And I figured flowers bring in birds, so I designed perennial borders supplemented with annuals that I start from seed."

Dolores' landscape boasts gardens galore, a 20-foot waterfall cascading down the bluff into a pond, and a smaller koi pond (pictured at left).

"I am not an expert, but I really do try to think like a hummingbird," she says. "Each year they come in greater and greater numbers. They're like kamikazes, diving and flitting all around you."

Dolores shares views of these avian acrobatics during the Henderson Hummingbird Hurrah, a bird-banding and garden-tour event held in cooperation with the Henderson Chamber of Commerce and Audubon Minnesota that drew 2,000 visitors to her home in August 2009. Dolores also opens her gardens by appointment; contact her at 507-248-3824 or *dhagen@closingthegap.com*.

Lovebirds Flock to Wisconsin

It was a small wedding-shower gift that sparked Kathi and Michael Rock's love affair with hummingbirds. The present, a simple hummingbird feeder, eventually led the Madison, Wisconsin, couple to transform nearly two-thirds of their 1-acre city lot into a hummingbird haven.

"We decided to hang the feeder and see what happened," recalls Kathi. "That summer we saw a hummingbird. That got us researching and talking with people."

The couple put their newfound knowledge to work, removing trees and overgrown shrubs to let in the sunlight needed by nectar-rich plants.

"Every year we try out new plants that sometimes work and sometimes don't," Kathi says. "Our goals are to have as many different plant varieties as we can, and to have hummingbird plants blooming from early spring into fall."

The Rocks open their gardens by appointment and host an annual garden tour in mid-September, when dozens of southbound hummers flock to their yard. The couple also share their knowledge through a newsletter. Contact Kathi via e-mail for more information at *kathijr@yahoo.com*.

Alabama Ornithologists

Martha and Bob Sargent of Clay, Alabama, have planted nearly a third of an acre with hummingbirds in mind. These self-taught field ornithologists and founders of a non-profit hummingbird study group, who've become nationally recognized experts and banders, experiment with blooms of all colors to attract hummers.

"We band 800 new birds every summer," says Bob. "Last year we put out 60 feeders through summer and fall, and so many hummingbirds visited that we had to refill the feeders every day."

Hummingbirds on their way north visit the Sargents in March. From July through September they explode on the scene, as adults and hatchlings return south.

Bob and Martha share their gardens by appointment. You can reach them at *rubythroat@aol.com* or 205-681-2888. Visit the Hummer/Bird Study Group at *hummingbirdsplus.org* for banding events.

110

hummer happenings

Hummingbird activity heats up with these reader stories.

Garden Buddies

I love the hummingbirds that visit me each year from April through September. One year, I was outside when I noticed one of those fliers perched on a plastic hummingbird yard stake.

That evening, I retired to the patio armed with a camera and tripod. My patience finally paid off when a little hummingbird flew over at just the right moment (above). I could not have planned a better photo if I had tried. **—HOLLY McKINNEY,** *Bend, Oregon*

Rewarding Rescue

While working at an airplane hangar in southeast Kansas, I noticed something across the room. At first I thought it was a falling leaf, but it occurred to me that leaves shouldn't be falling from our airplanes, so I went over to check it out. A beautiful male ruby-throated hummingbird was looking up at me from the floor with his wings spread.

After half an hour he hadn't moved, and his head and bill were resting on the floor. I nudged him with my pen to see if he was alive. He was! So I made him a cup of sugar water, lifted his head and got him to drink. Within an hour, he had flown out the door.

Three or four weeks later, I heard a wasplike buzzing near my ear. It was a hummingbird! It flew circles around my head before landing on my computer screen to look at me. Then it hovered around my shoulders for a bit before flying out the door.

I'll never be 100 percent sure, but I believe it was the same little bird I saved. God has created some amazing and marvelous things. Those hummers are one of the neatest. We're definitely putting out more hummingbird feeders at my house!

—WENDELL H. LAURIE
Quapaw, Oklahoma

Under Attack

A few years ago we had a house guest from Samoa. He adapted well to Southern California traffic and huge shopping malls, but then one day he was in the front yard admiring the flower garden when he came into the house, frantic. "There's a killer bee with a 2-inch-long stinger after me!" he shouted.

He was visibly upset, yelling that there wasn't anything like that in Samoa, so we went outside to do a little investigating. It didn't take too long to find out that the killer bee he was referring to was actually a hummingbird. After a while, he came to love those beautiful hummingbirds, too.

—DOT SAURER, *Santee, California*

Hot Pursuit

These sweet little birds entertained us every morning as we ate breakfast on our deck. We'd linger after our meal, talking and taking pictures before we adjourned indoors to the air conditioning.

—GINI SUNNERGREN, *Sparks, Nevada*

Bathing Beauty

Last spring I was working in the yard when I heard what sounded like a miniature grass edger. I turned around, and saw a hummingbird I'd never seen. I'm not sure if it was a rufous or an Allen's hummingbird, but it was gorgeous. The little flier came every day around the same time to bathe in our St. Francis fountain. I really wanted to get a good photo, so I sat for hours. My patience paid off, and I finally got the perfect shot.

—MISSY MORRILL
Newark, California

Editor's Note: Great photo, Missy! It puzzled us, too. Rufous and Allen's hummingbirds look nearly identical.

Human Perch

A couple of years ago, I was working the night shift. Every morning when I came home, I would watch the hummingbirds whiz around the feeder right beside me. One morning, my mom decided to stand by the feeder and hold a smaller feeder, just to see what the hummingbird would do. To our surprise, it stopped at the feeder she was holding.

I wanted to see if I could take it a step further, so I held out my finger and waited. Within half an hour, I was blessed with a visit from a hummingbird. It was such a strange experience. You could hardly feel the hummingbird on you, but you could definitely feel the breeze from the beating wings. What a joy! Here's the picture (right) from that day. It was an amazing experience to have that little flier so up close and personal.

—**BILLIE JENKINS**, *Troy, Virginia*

To the Rescue

One of the male ruby-throated hummingbirds I'd been feeding showed up on the floor of my equipment shop one day. He was weak and covered with spider webbing and dust. Wanting to help out, I took him to the feeder and gently inserted his bill into one of the feeder ports.

He showed no signs of movement, but after a few seconds his head bobbed as if he were sipping the sugar water. His eyes opened and he became more alert.

I cleaned the webbing from his wings and feet, using a teasing needle to remove the mess one strand at a time. This time at the feeder, he was able to clasp onto the perch and support his own weight. I gingerly guided his head and bill to a port, where he fed. Finally, he fluttered his wings, and after a final sip, the revived hummingbird flew to the nearest tree. It was such a great feeling to see a wonderful creature restored to his natural condition. —**WADE SNYDER**
Daniels, West Virginia

A Bright Bulb

Every year, my daughter and husband have a robin that nests on the light fixture near the entrance of their home. One year, they were surprised to find this additional nester on the lightbulb in the carport. My son-in-law took this picture of the mother bird on the nest. Later, three youngsters hatched.

—**ELEANOR HAMMONDS**, *San Antonio, Texas*

hummingbird
helpers from the house

These ordinary household objects can be turned into extraordinary hummingbird accessories.

Peanut butter lid. Bonnie Hutson of Independence, Missouri, sent this clever idea. Drill a hole in the center of a peanut butter lid. Attach a J bolt to one side and an eyebolt to the other. You'll have an instant ant moat!

Sugar. Make sugar water—four parts water to one part sugar. Hummers always come back for this sweet treat.

Wine bottle. Clean it out, fill it with sugar water and then attach a hummingbird feeding tube (search *amazon.com* to find some). Voilà!

Red ribbon. A little red goes a long way in attracting hummingbirds, especially when it's early in the season.

Rice, Sand or Popcorn. Add a little bit of one of these to your hummingbird feeder, along with some water. Then shake. You'll have a cleaner feeder in no time.

Cooking spray. Many readers swear by this. Just spraying some on your hummingbird feeder makes it too slippery for ants to cross.

Buttons or beads. Add a few to your sugar water. You'll be able to tell at a glance how low your supply is and when you need to refill.

Vinegar. You're guaranteed to have a clean feeder when you wash it with vinegar and water.

Pipe cleaners. These are perfect for cleaning those hard-to-reach spots of a sugar-water feeder.

Coat hangers. Add a few around your feeders to give hummingbirds plenty of places to perch.

no more ANTS!

did you know?

Impress your friends with these little-known facts about hummingbirds.

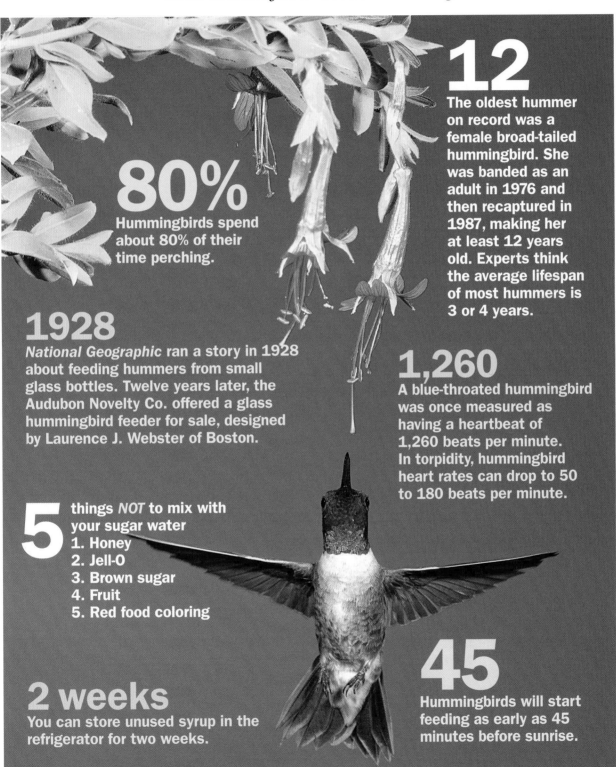

80%
Hummingbirds spend about 80% of their time perching.

12
The oldest hummer on record was a female broad-tailed hummingbird. She was banded as an adult in 1976 and then recaptured in 1987, making her at least 12 years old. Experts think the average lifespan of most hummers is 3 or 4 years.

1928
National Geographic ran a story in 1928 about feeding hummers from small glass bottles. Twelve years later, the Audubon Novelty Co. offered a glass hummingbird feeder for sale, designed by Laurence J. Webster of Boston.

1,260
A blue-throated hummingbird was once measured as having a heartbeat of 1,260 beats per minute. In torpidity, hummingbird heart rates can drop to 50 to 180 beats per minute.

5 things *NOT* to mix with your sugar water
1. Honey
2. Jell-O
3. Brown sugar
4. Fruit
5. Red food coloring

2 weeks
You can store unused syrup in the refrigerator for two weeks.

45
Hummingbirds will start feeding as early as 45 minutes before sunrise.

Facts provided by *hummingbirds.net*.

Ruby-throated hummingbird
Photo by Tim Fitzharris

Ruby-throated hummingbird
Photo by Anthony Frascella

Anna's hummingbird
Photo by Rocky Richardson

Black-chinned hummingbird
Photo by Larry Ditto / KAC Productions

Beautiful Blooms

Searching for a plant that's ideal for attracting birds and butterflies, or a colorful flower for your shade garden? Read on for some of our favorite plant picks from the year.

Dynamic Duos **120**

Top 10: Plants You Can't Kill **126**

Winter Wonders **130**

Top 10: Spring-Blooming Shrubs **134**

Gardening in Harmony **138**

Top 10: Colorful Shade Plants **140**

Second Chance Garden **144**

Green Garden Trends **148**

Photos of the Year **150**

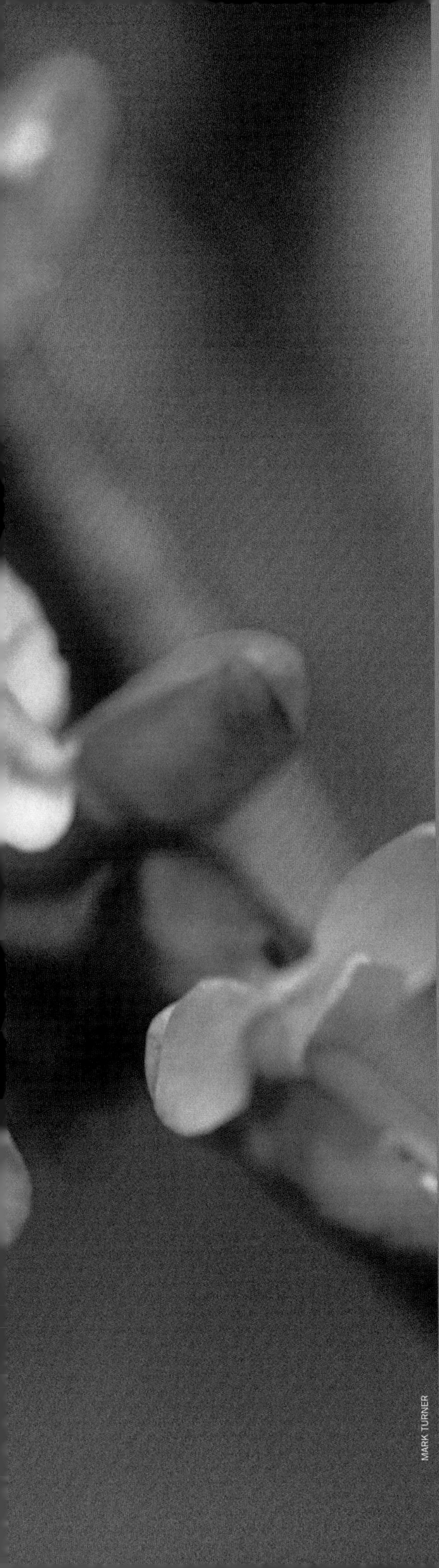

MARK TURNER

House wren
amid
hollyhocks

dynamic
Duos

Make the most of your outdoor space.
These multipurpose plants attract both
birds and butterflies.

By Kris Wetherbee

I'm always multitasking. So I thought, why can't plants? My yard is filled with plants that benefit wildlife. But why should I choose a plant that entices only one kind of visitor when others have multiple benefits?

Hollyhocks, for instance, attract butterflies with their nectar-rich blooms and also serve as caterpillar host plants for painted lady butterflies. (And they even offer good cover for birds, as you can see with the wren peeking out from the birdhouse on the previous page.)

Another plant that doubles the appeal is bachelor's buttons (*Centaurea cyanus*). This annual flower is popular for its nectar flowers and subsequent seed heads that appeal to many birds, including finches, buntings and sparrows.

When you really want to pack in the appeal, go for plants that offer triple the attraction. For example, look for plants such as cosmos and cleome. They offer nectar-rich blooms for hummingbirds and butterflies, seed heads that are a food

Bachelor's buttons

multipurpose trees & shrubs

Dogwood

(*Cornus* species, Zones 2 to 9)
Nectar flowers for butterflies; summer or fall berries for backyard birds such as robins, bluebirds and towhees; summer shelter; nesting site; caterpillar host plant for spring azure blue.

Fringe tree

(*Chionanthus* species, Zones 3 to 10)
Nectar flowers for butterflies; fruit eaten by more than 75 species of birds in late summer through fall; summer shelter; caterpillar host plant for hawk moths.

Redbud

(*Cercis* species, Zones 4 to 10)
Nectar flowers attract hummingbirds, butterflies such as hairstreaks, and other pollinating insects; seeds appeal to chickadees, American goldfinches and other seed-eating birds; nuthatches and woodpeckers eat bark insects from tree; summer shelter; caterpillar host plant for the Henry's elfin.

Cleome with female ruby-throated hummingbird

Elderberry

(*Sambucus* species, Zones 3 to 9)
Nectar flowers for hummingbirds, swallowtail and hairstreak butterflies, and various beneficial insects; summer-to-autumn berries appeal to a wide range of bird species; shelter site; nesting site.

Lavender

(*Lavandula* species, Zones 4 to 11)
Nectar flowers attract skippers, painted ladies and other butterfly species and pollinators; birds such as finches eat seed heads in early fall and winter; summer shelter; used as nesting material.

Viburnum

(*Viburnum* species, Zones 2 to 9)
Nectar flowers attract butterflies, some moths and beneficial insects; summer-to-winter fruit brings in a variety of birds; shelter and nesting site; caterpillar host plant for the spring azure blue butterfly as well as the sphinx and hummingbird moths.

source for a variety of birds, and shelter sites for juncos and other ground scratchers.

Other triple-threat players include plants such as verbena and penstemon that dish up food for caterpillars as host plants, attract butterflies and hummingbirds with nectar, and then bring in birds with tasty seed heads.

Roses are another prime example of plants with multiple benefits. Butterflies feed on their nectar flowers, and the hips feed many species of birds. In addition, some roses function as nesting sites, and most offer great summer shelter.

You get the picture. A backyard with a variety of plants attracts more wildlife, but a backyard filled with dynamic duos and other multipurpose plants gives you even more bang for the buck and more wildlife appeal for the space. So make the most of your plant selection and grow a garden for nature today.

tips
for putting it all together

● Group plants according to their needs for light, soil and moisture.
● Buy odd numbers of the same plant and group them together in a naturalistic way. Large shrubs, trees and specimen plants are the exception.
● Grow perennials and annuals in masses, whether by color, vegetative type or plant type. This brings a sense of harmony to the garden and is more likely to attract the attention of birds and butterflies.
● Maximize the space by featuring plants that vary in color, height and season of bloom. This creates a year-round habitat with different foraging and shelter opportunities.
● Include evergreen combinations that also provide food and shelter in winter.

multipurpose blooms

Aster

Chrysanthemum

Clematis

Coreopsis

Cosmos

Coneflower

Goldenrod

Honeysuckle

Milkweed

Penstemon

Verbena

Virginia creeper

Yarrow

Zinnia

Monarch on verbena

Redbud trees attract seed-eating birds. In addition, they provide excellent nesting sites for birds such as this Baltimore oriole.

Coneflower

1

plants you can't kill

They're tough as nails and pretty, too.

As gardeners, we're constantly faced with challenges: plants that won't bloom, flowers that die from a late frost, droughts that wipe out entire beds.

Gardening definitely has its fair share of difficulties, so every once in a while it's nice to have plants that require little maintenance. Even better—grow plants you can't kill!

Sure, spraying these all-stars with weed killer would probably lead to their demise. But for the most part, these are hardy, maintenance-free picks that work well in any North American backyard.

So are you ready to turn your black thumb into a green thumb? Get planting with these top picks.

Cosmos

2

Daylily

3

Hens-and-chicks

4

Yarrow

5

Hosta

6

Sedum

7

Zinnia

8

Petunia

9

Yucca

10

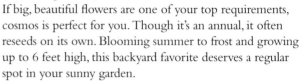

1 Coneflower

(Echinacea, Zones 3 to 9)

Coneflowers have become a garden staple for their easygoing nature. Growing 2 to 5 feet high and 2 feet wide, they are the perfect companion plant in just about any garden. They require well-drained soil but will thrive in full sun as well as partial shade. Known for attracting birds, bees and butterflies, coneflowers also make lovely cut blooms.

Why we love it: The coneflower is the low-maintenance star of nature-friendly gardens. It comes in many colors, and it's easy to find one you—and the birds—will love.

2 Cosmos

(Cosmos bipinnatus)

If big, beautiful flowers are one of your top requirements, cosmos is perfect for you. Though it's an annual, it often reseeds on its own. Blooming summer to frost and growing up to 6 feet high, this backyard favorite deserves a regular spot in your sunny garden.

Why we love it: It's easy to grow from seed. So for a couple of bucks, you'll have a gorgeous show in a single season.

5 Yarrow

(Achillea, Zones 3 to 9)

These easy-care, long-lasting flowers come into their own once summer is on its way. They grow 6 inches to 4 feet tall and 18 to 24 inches wide, in yellow, white, red and pink. Well-suited to most growing conditions, yarrows provide a long season of bloom. They're a good cutting flower, too. Avoid seedy varieties that may require a bit of weeding to keep contained.

Why we love it: This plant is heat- and drought-tolerant and can survive on benign neglect.

6 Hosta

(Hosta, Zones 3 to 8)

Easy-to-grow hosta is a must for shade gardens. The beautiful foliage comes in a wealth of colors, textures, sizes and shapes, growing 4 inches to 3 feet high and 6 inches to 6 feet wide. In summer, hosta blooms in purple, white or lavender. Divide in spring or late summer to early fall. Hostas like moist ground, but be careful not to overwater.

Why we love it: The ultimate low-care shade plant, hosta comes in endless varieties and colors. It also can be easily divided—perfect for the budget-minded.

9 Petunia

(Petunia x *hybrida)*

Petunias have been around for decades, but the newer varieties have advanced in leaps and bounds. Days of deadheading and disease-prone plants are long gone. Nowadays, these beauties flourish in both full sun and partial shade without a lot of extra work. And you can find them in almost every color imaginable.

Why we love it: Even if you forget to water for a few days—it happens to everyone—these plants keep going.

10 Yucca

(Yucca filamentosa, Zones 4 to 11)

There's a good reason so many Southern gardeners use this as a backyard centerpiece. It's about as drought-tolerant as they come—and on top of that, it boasts beautiful white flowers amid its spiky leaves.

Why we love it: Both flowers and foliage come with this beauty. For a unique variety, look for the variegata cultivar. Its blue-green leaves with white edges are stunning.

3

Daylily
(*Hemerocallis,* Zones 3 to 10)

An excellent choice for a classic garden, daylilies can tolerate flooding, drought and salt and are often used for erosion control on steep hillsides. The pretty blooms come in every shade except blue and pure white; their distinctive trumpets may be triangular, circular, double, spidery or star-shaped. Daylilies grow 10 inches to 4 feet high and 1½ to 4 feet wide and do best in full sun to partial shade.

Why we love it: Some cultivars attract hummingbirds and butterflies. A plant that is best divided every three to five years, the daylily is perfect to share with friends.

4

Hens-and-chicks
(*Sempervivum tectorum,* Zones 3 to 8)

The only way to kill this succulent is by being too kind with overwatering. This perennial is perfect for rock gardens. It grows 3 to 6 inches tall and up to 20 inches wide and blooms in summer. For best results, plant in well-drained soil that gets full sun to light shade.

Why we love it: This low grower also works wonders in containers. Since it doesn't have a deep root system, you can plant it somewhere fun. Try growing it in an old birdbath or shoe.

7

Sedum
(*Sedum* species, Zones 3 to 10)

Take a close look and you'll see this plant's star-shaped blooms, similar to a pentas. With yellow, orange, red, pink or white flowers, it grows from 2 inches up to 2 feet high and wide. You can grow some species as ground cover, while others make good border plants.

Why we love it: Hello, butterflies! If you want flying flowers in your yard, this plant is a slam dunk.

8

Zinnia
(*Zinnia*)

With new heat-, drought- and disease-resistant plants on the market, there's never been a better time to grow zinnias. This annual grows up to 3 feet high, with blooms that last until the first frost. For the newest varieties from seed, check your local nursery or favorite garden catalog. If you don't find what you're looking for, order online.

Why we love it: You'll save tons of money growing these from seed. Start seeds indoors, or sow outdoors about ¼ inch deep after the threat of frost has passed.

CRABAPPLE, BAILEY NURSERIES

Can't-Kill
Trees & Shrubs

If you're in the market for a larger addition, try one of these resilient picks.

Crabapple. It offers beautiful blooms in spring and tasty berries from fall through winter. Plus, you can find sturdy disease-resistant varieties with small persistent (not messy) fruit these days.

Spirea. This shrub is often overused in landscapes, but there's a reason. Add it to your yard to find out what the fuss is all about.

Juniper. Don't let its ordinary look fool you. This age-old favorite is hard as nails in the garden.

winter
wonders

From sparkling seed heads to fiery blades, ornamental grasses provide food and shelter for winged wildlife.

By Kris Wetherbee, Oakland, Oregon

Grasses are one of the essential plants for any garden, and not just from a design perspective. They also provide a living habitat, offering food and shelter to a variety of birds.

Toward summer's end, many grasses send up graceful plumage of varying colors into late fall. Hues change as the air cools, brightening the horizon with autumn reds and yellows.

As winter descends, with dawn frosts and blankets of snow, ornamental grasses are once again transformed into shimmering splendor.

ALAN AND LINDA DETRICK

Wildlife Appeal

The seed heads of many grasses, such as Japanese silver grass (*Miscanthus sinensis*), serve as a fall and winter food source for a variety of visitors, including purple finches, sparrows, juncos and goldfinches.

Grasses also provide low cover for ground-frequenting birds such as towhees, sparrows and quail. Japanese forest grass, prairie dropseed and many of the taller varieties offer great winter havens. Then, come spring, birds use their dried leaves and plumes to build their nests.

Grasses in the Landscape

Ease of care, wildlife appeal and year-round good looks virtually assure the success of modern ornamental grasses. Sizes range from ground-hugging clumps to impressive displays towering 14 feet or more. And their myriad of textures, shapes and hues mean endless design possibilities.

Grasses work well as ground covers, edgings or accents. Combine them with perennials, annuals, flowering bulbs and shrubs to add textural interest. Group them together to form natural screens or attractive windbreaks, or feature taller, statelier species as dramatic focal points. However you use them, they can turn your garden into a four-season showplace.

Did You Know?
Butterflies, too, seek shelter in grasses. Certain species of skippers favor them as host plants.

great *grasses*

Take a look at six sensational grasses that are beautiful year-round.

A, B, C, E, F: RICK WETHERBEE; D, RDA-GID

A. Blue oat grass
(*Helictotrichon sempervirens*)
Striking contrast between bright silvery-blue foliage and wispy, straw-colored plumes that grow to 3 feet tall. Zone 3.

B. Feather reed grass
(*Calamagrostis* x *acutiflora*)
Upright grass 2 to 5 feet tall. Standing plumes to 6 feet in white, pink or red, changing to golden tan in fall. Zone 3.

C. Fountain grass
(*Pennisetum* species)
Graceful grass grows in fountain shapes from 18 inches to 5 feet tall. Furry plumes resemble foxtails in shades of green, pink or purple that rise above green or purple leaves. Annual and perennial species available.

D. Switchgrass
(*Panicum virgatum*)
Airy flowerheads hover over foliage of greens, blues or reds. Yellow fall color gives way to an attractive beige for winter. Reseeds readily; consider cultivars for small spaces. Zone 3.

E. Japanese silver grass
(*Miscanthus sinensis*)
Graceful group of grasses growing 2 to 6 feet tall. Autumn foliage from yellow to claret, with showy silvery, pinkish or bronze plumes that last well into winter. Zone 4.

F. Mexican feather grass
(*Stipa tenuissima*)
Fountains of finely textured, silky green leaves growing to 2 feet. Straw-colored plumes grace the fall and winter landscape. Evergreen in cool winter climates. Zone 6.

Why grow grasses? Grasses are drought-tolerant and require little or no feeding. If it's needed, spread a 1- to 2-inch layer of garden compost to provide ample nutrients and keep grasses looking their best.

Lilac

1

spring-blooming shrubs

Enjoy the scents and sights of these lush early bloomers.

By Crystal Rennicke

As winter ends, gardeners look for hopeful signs that spring is on its way. Early-blooming shrubs are a perfect awakening for a winter-weary backyard. If you're looking to give your backyard a boost of color come spring, incorporate one or more of these 10 favorite shrubs into your landscape.

Vernal witchhazel
2

Weigela
3

Cornelian cherry dogwood
4

Flowering quince
5

Bridal wreath spirea
6

Azalea
7

Nanking cherry
8

Crapemyrtle
9

Forsythia
10

1
Lilac

(Syringa vulgaris, Zones 3 to 8)

The distinctive scent and lovely blooms of lilac, which come in lavender, white, pink, magenta, blue and bicolors, have made it one of the most popular flowering shrubs in North America. With sizes from 4 to 30 feet high and 5 to 22 feet wide to choose from, it's easy to bring the delightful fragrance to any landscape. Try Ludwig Spaeth for later blooms or the new Bloomerang® reblooming lilac.

2
Vernal witchhazel

(Hamamelis vernalis, Zones 4 to 8)

Grown for its brightly colored spring blooms and spicy fragrance, this is a beautiful shrub that bears yellow, orange or red flowers in late winter. A slow grower, the mature plant grows 8 to 10 feet tall and wide. For fragrant blooms in winter, try forcing stem cuttings indoors. Lombart's Weeping has spreading branches that reach 6 feet tall and 10 feet wide.

5
Flowering quince

(Chaenomeles speciosa, Zones 4 to 8)

Grown for its stunning spring flowers and edible fruit, this is a favorite landscape shrub. Showy pink, red, orange or white flowers emerge in early spring, and green-yellow fruit can be used in jellies when ripe. Its foliage opens red-bronze, then turns dark green in summer. A vigorous, spreading shrub, flowering quince will grow to 8 feet tall and 15 feet wide. Cardinalis bears crimson flowers; Dwarf Orange is a bit more compact with orange flowers.

6
Bridal wreath spirea

(Spiraea, Zones 3 to 8)

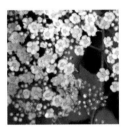

Depending on species, several spring-blooming spireas are known as Bridal Wreath. An old-fashioned favorite, it is covered with tiny, white, roselike flowers in spring. In summer, the 6- to 10-foot-tall shrub has oval green leaves that turn bronze-yellow to red in autumn. Plant it in full sun, mulch around it to keep it healthy and prune in late winter for a beautiful spring show. If you're looking for a compact shrub 3 to 5 feet tall, try Snowmound or Snow White.

9
Crapemyrtle

(Lagerstroemia indica, Zones 7 to 9)

Transition from spring to summer with crapemyrtle. A Southern favorite, crapemyrtle has beautiful white, pink, red or purple flowers that emerge in spring and last through autumn. Many new varieties are bred to resist powdery mildew and have eye-catching gray-and-brown peeling bark. This handsome shrub grows to 15 to 30 feet tall and 6 to 15 feet wide. Natchez grows to 20 feet tall and wide with white flowers; for a more compact grower at 7 to 8 feet tall and wide, try Seminole, which produces mid-pink flowers.

10
Forsythia

(Forsythia, Zones 3 to 8)

When this shrub blooms, you know warmer weather is on the way. Forsythia is one of the first plants to flower in spring, when its golden bell-shaped blossoms are a welcome sight. Once the shrubs have bloomed, and if they're more than 3 years old, get out the pruning shears and cut the very oldest branches down near the ground in order to encourage new shoots for next year.

3 Weigela

(*Weigela*, Zones 4 to 9)

For a pretty shrub with interest from early spring through fall, try weigela in your borders and beds. Hummingbirds love the tubular pink, white or red flowers that emerge in spring. Its foliage is eye-catching throughout the growing season, and in some varieties changes color in fall. Sizes range from 2 to 8 feet tall and wide. For a compact shrub with bold pink flowers and burgundy fall foliage, try Fine Wine. For yellow flowers, try *Weigela subsessilis* 'Canary'.

4 Cornelian cherry dogwood

(*Cornus mas*, Zones 4 to 8)

Tiny yellow flower clusters appear on the branches of this shrub in early spring. A larger shrub or small ornamental tree, Cornelian cherry has a mature size of 15 feet tall and 20 feet wide. In summer, immature green fruit turns bright red and is a treat for birds. For a more upright and formal growth habit, try Golden Glory, which grows to 25 feet tall and 15 feet wide, with dense flowering.

7 Azalea

(*Rhododendron*, Zones 4 to 8)

Like its relative rhododendron, azalea is a prolific spring bloomer. Its flower clusters, which bloom in white, yellow, orange, pink, red and other colors, are smaller than the rhododendron's but just as showy. Depending on the cultivar, azaleas will grow 1 to 15 feet high. For best results, add an inch-deep layer of mulch around the base of the shrub. Try Palestrina for a compact, 4-foot-high shrub with white blooms. Encore azaleas bloom in spring, summer and fall.

8 Nanking cherry

(*Prunus tomentosa*, Zones 2 to 7)

A hardy, fast-growing shrub, Nanking cherry produces fragrant white flowers in spring. A larger shrub or small ornamental tree, it grows to 6 to 10 feet tall and wide. After the spring bloom, small cherry-shaped fruits form, a favorite of many songbirds. Use in the landscape for a hedge, border or specimen planting. White Nanking cherry (*Prunus tomentosa* 'Leucocarpa') produces white fruit in summer.

Spring-Blooming Bulbs

Looking for more wow this spring? Plant these bulbs in fall for a spectacular show in spring.

Tulip. A classic favorite, tulips come in so many shapes and colors. Try the long-lived *Tulipa tarda*, which has up to five yellow-and-white flowers on a stem.

Hyacinth. This favorite is loved for its fragrant spring show. Try Hollyhocks with its double raspberry-red flowers.

Checkered lily. Purple, pinkish purple or white checkered flowers are a delight in spring gardens. Try Charon with deep-purple blooms.

Snowdrop. One of the first bulbs to bloom, often when snow still covers the ground. Try *Galanthus elwesii* for larger flowers.

gardening *in harmony*

Grow your plants and eat them, too, by mixing veggies and blooms.

By Melinda Myers

Growing vegetables is more popular than ever, but that doesn't mean you have to give up the space of your flower garden.

Long gone are the days of banishing your veggies and herbs to the back corner of your yard because they're not "pretty." Instead, try growing them front and center among the flowers in your garden or containers.

Ready for Sun

I've been using herbs and veggies to brighten my landscape and add fresh-from-the-garden flavor to my meals for more than 20 years. Including them among my blooms allows me to squeeze edible plants into my small-space landscape while still growing other species.

As always, start by matching your plants to the growing conditions of your area. Most herbs and vegetables do best with at least eight hours of sunlight a day.

Tomatoes, peppers, squash and other plants that produce flowers and fruit do best in eight to 12 hours of sun. Beets, radishes, carrots and other root crops can tolerate a bit of shade. Just make sure they receive at least four to six hours of sunlight. Greens such as lettuce and spinach are the most shade tolerant. They can grow well with a mere four hours of sunlight, or a day filled with bright, indirect light.

Fabulous Foliage

When planning your garden, look for herb and vegetable varieties with colorful foliage or fruits. I like bright-light Swiss chard with colorful red, orange and yellow stems. It works perfectly as a vertical accent in a pot, or as a foliage accent in flower gardens.

One of my favorite spring combinations is Swiss chard, colorful leaf lettuce, pansies (they're edible, too) and a trailing vinca or ivy. Another good choice is tricolor sage, whose cream, green and purple-pink variegated leaves work well with purple heliotrope, Persian shield and other purple and pink blooms.

The dark foliage of bull's blood beet also harmonizes with flowers. I first saw this heirloom planted at Seed Savers Exchange (*seedsavers.org*). They used it as an edging plant mixed with Argentine verbena around the base of a tepee support covered with scarlet runner beans.

138

Time to Harvest

Don't forget about herbs. Try using the fine texture of dill or fennel as a filler among pepper, kale and basil plants. You don't need a lot of space to grow these, and it's great to have fresh herbs on hand.

Once your garden is in full force, don't forget to keep harvesting regularly. This will keep the vegetables producing and looking good longer. And once a short-season crop like lettuce or beets has been harvested, be prepared to fill the void with a late-season flower or vegetable.

You really can have your plants and eat them, too. All it takes is a little planning!

10 best veggies for kids to grow

1. **SUGAR SNAP PEAS.** Kids love to eat them fresh off the vine.

2. **LETTUCE.** Easy-to-grow lettuce comes in lots of cool color varieties.

3. **RADISHES.** Within a month, these fast growers are ready to pick. Just for giggles, try red, white and purple varieties.

4. **CARROTS.** Quick-growing carrots are perfect for short attention spans.

5. **POTATOES.** Kids really dig potatoes, which are as much fun to harvest as to eat.

6. **GREEN BEANS.** The big seeds are fun and easy to plant.

7. **CHERRY TOMATOES.** Little hands love to pick these tiny fruits.

8. **PUMPKINS.** Plant a smaller variety, like Jack Be Little, for your smaller helpers.

9. **SUNFLOWERS.** These beauties take off without much work, and come in tall or small varieties. Plus, it's fun to harvest the seeds, or leave out the seed heads to attract birds.

10. **BROCCOLI.** Like many veggies, garden-fresh broccoli tastes sweeter than store-bought.

Celosia, broccoli and lettuce

Sunflowers and corn

Chili peppers and perennials

Lobelia and lettuce

Astilbe

1

colorful shade plants

Got shade? Brighten it up with these colorful perennials.

By Crystal Rennicke

If you thought you were doomed to a colorless panorama because of your shady yard, think again! Embrace your shady spots. There are plenty of colorful perennials that can brighten lackluster places.

These 10 perennials were chosen for their easy-growing natures and ability to bring much-needed color to even the shadiest spots. Some are considered ground covers for their spreading habits and ability to fill in underneath trees or on shaded slopes. Others work well in beds and borders that need a little color boost. And as a bonus, most have beautiful flowers as well as foliage.

Brunnera
2

Hakone grass
3

Rodger's flower
4

Lungwort
5

Toad lily
6

European ginger
7

Coral bells
8

Goatsbeard
9

Solomon's seal
10

1

Astilbe

(*Astilbe,* Zones 3 to 9)

For many, a shade garden would not be complete without the feathery blooms of astilbe. This perennial serves as a great border plant with showy wands of colorful blooms that sway on slender stalks in summer. The ferny foliage will add interest even when the plant is not in bloom. Growing 8 to 48 inches high and wide, astilbe will add dense color to your shade garden. For best results, divide and replant in early spring every three or four years.

Why we love it: Graceful feathery tufts of flowers come in bright colors and attract bees, birds and butterflies.

2

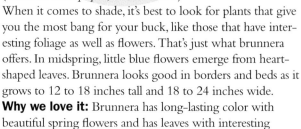

Brunnera

(*Brunnera macrophylla,* Zones 3 to 8)

When it comes to shade, it's best to look for plants that give you the most bang for your buck, like those that have interesting foliage as well as flowers. That's just what brunnera offers. In midspring, little blue flowers emerge from heart-shaped leaves. Brunnera looks good in borders and beds as it grows to 12 to 18 inches tall and 18 to 24 inches wide.

Why we love it: Brunnera has long-lasting color with beautiful spring flowers and has leaves with interesting texture and color.

5

Lungwort

(*Pulmonaria,* Zones 2 to 8)

In early spring, the brilliant blue, pink or white flowers of lungwort bloom despite a late chill. The rough leaves, spotted or plain, remain handsome through the season into winter. Plant this weed-discouraging ground cover in borders or as an edging or accent plant. It's 6 to 12 inches tall and easy!

Why we love it: Colorful foliage and flowers add interest all season long.

6

Toad lily

(*Tricyrtis,* Zones 4 to 9)

Its unique, orchidlike blooms in white, mauve and yellow earn toad lily a closer look. Perfect for a small, woodland shade garden, toad lily grows 1 to 2 feet wide and 1 to 3 feet tall. It's easy to grow, drought-tolerant and resistant to deer.

Why we love it: Toad lily blooms just as the rest of the garden is winding down for fall. Plus, those spotted blooms are definitely unique!

9

Goatsbeard

(*Aruncus,* Zones 3 to 7)

This regal shade dweller makes a statement, reaching up to 6 feet tall with big, creamy white flower plumes reminiscent of a large astilbe. The ferny, deep-green leaves are attractive, too. Also called bride's feathers, goatsbeard blooms in early summer, usually around June. It loves moist soil.

Why we love it: Goatsbeard is a dramatic shade plant with delicate flowers.

10

Solomon's seal

(*Polygonatum,* Zones 3 to 9)

Its tall, dramatic foliage is a main attraction, but the little bell-like flowers (usually white, sometimes purple-pink) that dangle under the stems in spring are enchanting, too. Easy to grow, Solomon's seal is an elegant shade plant that grows 4 inches to 6 feet high and 10 to 24 inches wide.

Why we love it: Slowly covering ground in shady spots, Solomon's seal adds height and grace to gardens in spring.

3 Hakone grass

(*Hakonechloa macra,* Zones 5 to 9)
Ornamental grasses typically need sun to thrive, but hakone grass is made for the shade. Growing 12 to 14 inches tall and 12 to 16 inches wide, hakone grass works well in beds and borders and on slopes. It has attractive foliage, with bright yellow and green stripes, and its foliage takes on a reddish-pink tinge in fall. Give it extra TLC to establish it in the first few years. It likes its soil moist but not wet.
Why we love it: The Perennial Plant Association chose golden hakone grass as the 2009 Perennial Plant of the Year.

4 Rodger's flower

(*Rodgersia,* Zones 5 to 8)
Rodger's flower has large, interesting-shaped leaves that are green or bronze-tinged and heavily veined and often turn reddish in fall. The large, astilbe-like plumes of tiny flowers are an attractive bonus. Plant it in rain gardens or near streams or ponds. It grows 3 to 6 feet tall and 2 to 3 feet wide, with white, rose pink, red or yellow flowers.
Why we love it: This hidden gem attracts butterflies and has striking bold foliage and feathery flowers.

7 European ginger

(*Asarum europaeum,* Zones 4 to 7)
This ground cover has beautiful, glossy, heart-shaped leaves that spread rapidly throughout the shade garden. In spring, it bears purplish-maroon, bell-shaped blooms that are hidden in the foliage. Growing 4 to 10 inches tall and 6 to 12 inches wide, it will quickly become a favorite in the shade.
Why we love it: These shiny, beautiful evergreen leaves stay relatively pest-free.

8 Coral bells

(*Heuchera,* Zones 3 to 9)
Colorful foliage and dainty blooms make coral bells a must in a shady space. Bell-like blooms emerge in late spring and last through early summer on 8- to 18-inch plants. The striking foliage of coral bells comes in an assortment of colors: purple, red, black, silver, amber, orange and bronze, and some are evergreen through winter.
Why we love it: Coral bells will work in sun or shade, and its blooms attract hummingbirds.

Best Annuals
for the Shade

You don't have to give up your flowers to get cheery color in the shade. Use these top annuals in containers or to fill in spotty areas of your garden.

Coleus	Polka dot plant
Impatiens	Wishbone flower
Browallia	Begonia

chance garden

Sometimes it's not too late to grow what you really wanted.

By Melinda Myers

As summer fades, you realize it just wasn't quite long enough. If you're like me, you'll still have a gardening to-do list of things you didn't get around to during the peak of the season. Don't worry—there's still time to cross a few things off your list. Consider this your second chance.

Fall Veggies

Let's start with all those fresh vegetables you wanted to grow for your family. Our Southern gardening friends are used to planting many of their crops in the fall. But no matter where you live, you can still add to your fall harvest.

Start with a look at your weather and find out what the first average fall frost date is in your area. Then count the number of days left, and you can figure out what you can grow.

For example, even with a mere 45 days left until frost, you'll still have time to plant and harvest radishes, leaf lettuce, mustard greens, spinach, beets and onions. In fact, many crops, including lettuce, spinach, broccoli and cauliflower, taste better when harvested during cooler temperatures. These days, garden centers are helping out, too. Many provide transplants of fall vegetables to shorten the time between planting and harvest.

Extend the Season

If you're willing to put in a bit of extra effort, you can even extend the growing season past the first fall frost. For this, I like using floating row covers sold as Reemay, Harvest-Guard and Grass-Fast. These spun fabrics let air, light and water through while trapping the heat near the plant.

To use, loosely cover the plants with the fabric and anchor the edges with boards, stones or wire wickets. No construction needed! And you can leave them in place until you're ready to harvest or end the growing season.

Cold frames are another option for those good with a hammer and nails. With a bit of lumber, recycled window sash or plastic, you can

Row covers are a small but definitely worthwhile investment. They allow you to plant earlier in spring and harvest later in fall. Try brands like Reemay, Harvest-Guard and Grass-Fast.

extend your growing season in both spring and fall.

Perennial Perfection

Maybe your wish list includes a bit of long-term beautification. Fall is an ideal time for planting perennials. No matter where you live, plants suffer less transplant shock and need less water when planted in the warm soil and cooler weather of fall.

If you visit your favorite garden center or nursery, you might be surprised at what you find. Many have fresh shipments of plants arriving

Ornamental kale

throughout fall, providing healthy and attractive plants. Bargain hunters also love this time of year because many stores clear out their lots before winter, selling their plants at big discounts.

Bargain hunters also love this time of year because many stores clear out their lots before winter.

GET GROWING FASTER. Since lettuce is considered a cool-season crop, give it an early start indoors during summer. Then transplant it outside later when temps are a bit cooler.

Add Color With Containers

Adding fall containers is a great way to top off the growing season and add a bit of pizzazz to the landscape. For example, ornamental grasses, Swiss chard, asters, mums and other seasonal favorites provide nice vertical interest. Then add in cool-weather annuals like pansies, snapdragons, stocks, alyssum and ornamental cabbage or kale for a fabulous fall display.

Divide and Conquer

Fall is also a good time to dig and divide overgrown plants, especially spring bloomers. When you dig up overgrown perennials, keep as much of the root system intact as possible. Using a sharp knife, shovel or garden fork, divide the clump into two to six pieces. (The bigger the division, the bigger the impact will be in next year's garden. But that also means you'll be dividing sooner.)

Next, add a bit of compost, aged manure or other organic matter to the soil before planting. You can replant a piece of the division back in its original location. Use the extras to fill in voids in your garden, or share and trade with your gardening friends and neighbors.

Plant Trees and Shrubs

This is also a good time to add trees and shrubs to your landscape. Before you add them, make sure they have multiseason interest or function in your landscape. Flowers, fruits and colorful bark mean you'll enjoy year-round impact.

Increase your planting success with proper care. Plant trees with the root flare (the area where the roots curve away from the trunk) at or slightly above the soil surface. For shrubs, plant them with the crown (the place where roots meet the stem) at the soil line.

Water thoroughly at planting, and whenever the top few inches of soil are slightly moist, until the ground freezes. Add a few inches of shredded bark, wood chips or other organic mulch onto the soil around the trees and shrubs. This will help keep roots moist and soil temperatures stable, which aids winter survival.

Plan Ahead

Remember to use this time to plan ahead. Bulbs are a wonderful addition to any garden, so plant now to ensure gorgeous color in spring.

Don't let wildlife dissuade you from planting. Some smart, animal-resistant bulb choices are daffodils, hyacinths, fritillaria, grape hyacinths and squills.

Finally, if you're still feeling ambitious, get a jump on next year's gardening wish list. Start that new garden bed you've always wanted. Prepare the soil now, and come spring you're ready to plant. Or maybe you really wanted a new patio or deck. Roll up your sleeves or hire a professional now, and you'll be ready for the season.

Now is your chance to have the garden you really wanted. Don't let this second chance pass you by!

Be sure to check out the International Flower Bulb Center (*bulb.com*) for the best regional bulb selection and planting information to plan your backyard.

green *garden trends*

Recent reports about the latest trends in green gardening. By Melinda Myers

What's old is new again—and that goes for gardening, too. Each year, I visit a number of garden shows, everywhere from Seattle to Philadelphia, on my annual tour. There's a lot of talk about heirloom plants. And when old trends like this return, there's often a new twist or improvement to pique our interest or ease our work.

And so goes the green movement. Many of you have been influenced by this trend since the late '70s or early '80s, and some of the "new" garden ideas may seem like old news to you. But a closer look will reveal an update or innovation that makes it easier or more fun to go green.

A New Life

Gardeners and especially *Birds & Blooms* subscribers have always found creative ways of giving used items a second or third life. Examples of this repurposing are now filling display gardens and vendor booths in flower shows across the country.

If it can be planted in, it is. Chair planters are a perfect example. You've probably seen—and maybe even made—a planter from a pot of flowers placed in a broken-down chair. But creative gardeners have now been adding a new twist. For example, how about a seat cushion of hens-and-chicks, or a moss-covered recliner?

Here's another idea. Old musical instruments don't need to go to the recycling center. Convert them into decorative garden fountains and art.

Green Is the New Black

Large-scale environmental trends are also starting to move into our home landscapes. Green roofs, which are improving the environment in many communities, may not work for every homeowner. But never count out the creative gardener. Many have downsized the idea to fit their landscape with green-roof bird feeders, birdhouses, doghouses and garden sheds. One gardener transformed an old wishing well into a green accent, making a planter out of the well and installing a green roof on top.

Water conservation continues to be foremost in all of our minds. Rain barrels and rain harvesting systems are a growing part of the landscape. Gardeners, inventors and artists are helping to make them a beautiful part of the garden. One creative vendor that I saw wraps barrels in netting and grows annual vines to brighten up the view even more.

Eco-friendly furnishings and garden art can be found at every show. You can find Haitian art crafted from 50-gallon drums; light fixtures that were once vegetable cans and wine bottles; and bird feeders made from stray pieces of the family silver. Furniture and fencing take on a rustic look with twigs and branches used to create wattle fences, arbors and chairs.

New Plants and Pest Management

The edible landscape movement continues to grow, with gardeners always looking for new ways and places to grow vegetables: intensive planting, square-foot gardening, vegetables grown in containers and front yards. Many of the new decorative vegetable varieties—like Fairy Tale eggplant,

Bright Lights Swiss chard, Chinese Five Color pepper and Purple Passion asparagus—make edible gardening easy, attractive and fun.

Smaller-scale plants allow anyone to garden. The 16-inch-tall elf sunflower will fit in a window box, pot or garden. Lo and Behold noninvasive butterfly bush is great as a mass planting or alone in a pot.

Eco-friendly products are also growing in numbers. Environmentally friendly pest-management and plant-strengthening products made from plant oils, from plant proteins or from pest-killing fungi and bacteria make it easier to lend nature a hand when pests are wreaking havoc.

So are you inspired? Make room in your garden for something old, green, borrowed and new this year.

Flowering cherry tree
Photo by David Cavagnaro

California poppies
Photo by Tim Fitzharris

Hyacinths with late spring snow
Photo by Dennis Frates / Positive Images

Bee balm
*Photo by reader Jeni Albrecht
of Spokane, Washington*

Blue daisies
*Photo by reader Wendy Oster
of Downingtown, Pennsylvania*

RICHARD DAY / DAYBREAK IMAGERY

CHAPTER 6

Great Escapes

Want to get away? These destinations are some of the best places for birding and gardening across the country. Whether you want to stay close to home or are looking for an adventure, first check out these hot spots.

Rocky Mountain Escape **154**

Great Lakes Paradise **158**

Take Your Pick **162**

Traveling Light **168**

A Photographer's Dream **172**

Photos of the Year **176**

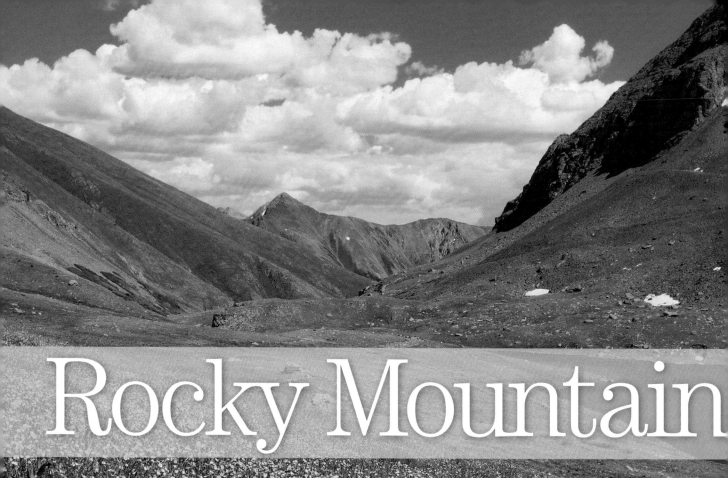

Rocky Mountain

The Colorado state
flower, Rocky Mountain
columbine

Better known for ski slopes and mountain views, Denver has another natural beauty hidden in the heart of downtown.

Denver Botanic Gardens has more than 34,000 plants, representing more than 9,000 species, in 23 acres, making it the sixth-largest botanic garden in the nation.

escape

Despite its mile-high climate, Denver sets a lofty standard for botanical gardens.

By Jacqueline DuPont

Sunset at Denver Botanic Gardens

High Altitude? No Problem!

When it comes to Denver's altitude, gardeners do have to make a few adjustments. The drier air, for instance, makes water evaporate more quickly. And the greater exposure to ultraviolet light can make plant colors fade.

But you wouldn't know high altitudes are any more difficult by looking at the gardens' alpine section. This internationally acclaimed specialty garden has more than 500 tons of rock amid its plants, making an ideal environment to withstand windy conditions with minimal water.

Besides the alpine area, other highlights of the Denver attraction are a traditional Japanese garden, a prairie garden, the waterlily collection and the tropical conservatory.

On the Cutting Edge

Special events and new exhibits are always opening at the gardens. The most recent addition is a children's garden where kids can climb, jump, run, dig and plant. This is a permanent feature, but be sure to check the website to learn about other seasonal activities, art shows and more.

May and June are peak months to visit the gardens, so start planning your visit to this alpine treasure soon. You can learn more at *botanicgardens.org* or 720-865-3500.

If you're not going to make it to Denver this year, take a look at some of these other rocky escapes instead.

Waterfall at The New York Botanical Garden

Annuals at Denver gardens

more lively alpine gardens

BETTY FORD ALPINE GARDENS • Vail, Colorado
At this lofty location, you'll find surprises around every corner. The expansive alpine rock area features everything from a waterfall and patio to a bog garden and aspen grove. And to top it off, there's no admission fee! Learn more at *bettyfordalpinegardens.org* or 970-476-0103.

MISSOURI BOTANICAL GARDEN • St. Louis, Missouri
Located on the grounds of the Missouri Botanical Garden are the Heckman rock garden and the Kassabaum dwarf conifer collection. This unique area features perennials native to Missouri and succulents in the West. All the plants here work well in rocky, alkaline soil, so if you have similar soil and are looking for recommendations, it's an excellent go-to source. Learn more at *mobot.org* or 314-577-5100.

OLBRICH BOTANICAL GARDENS • Madison, Wisconsin

Located in Wisconsin's capital city is Olbrich Botanical Gardens, named one of the 10 most inspiring gardens in North America by *Horticulture Magazine*. One of many highlights is a limestone-rich rock garden, home to lots of tough alpine plants. While in the area, you might also want to check out the rock garden at the Allen Centennial Gardens at the University of Wisconsin-Madison. Learn more about Olbrich at *olbrich.org* or 608-246-4550.

BELLEVUE BOTANICAL GARDEN • Bellevue, Washington

Just minutes from Seattle, the Bellevue Botanical Garden offers free admission and even free group tours if you request one ahead of time. Though the alpine area is relatively new to its landscape, you'll still enjoy the plants found in the 8,000-square-foot area, positioned among 800 tons of granite. Learn more at *bellevuebotanical.org* or 425-452-2750.

ATLANTA BOTANICAL GARDEN • Atlanta, Georgia

It's an alpine garden with a Southern twist! Since alpine plants won't grow in Georgia, the designers took the principles and aesthetics of a typical rock garden and used similar Southern plants instead. Gardeners who face hot, dry conditions will find lots of ideas here. Learn more at *atlantabotanicalgarden.org* or 404-876-5859.

THE NEW YORK BOTANICAL GARDEN • Bronx, New York

Waterfalls and streams sparkle amid primroses and woodland plants in the amazing 3-acre rock garden at The New York Botanical Garden. After extensive restoration, this garden boasts a riot of alpine flowers, many grown directly from seed that came from mountainous regions around the world. You'd be hard-pressed to find a more colorful rock garden in the country. Learn more at *nybg.org* or 718-817-8700.

UNIVERSITY OF BRITISH COLUMBIA BOTANICAL GARDEN • Vancouver, British Columbia

Visitors can walk among plants from the Andes, coastal Morocco, the Canary Islands and Asia Minor. On a sunny southwest-facing slope, designers have combined rocky outcrops and soil mixes to simulate the varied conditions in which alpine plants naturally grow. The garden features slow-growing dwarf conifers as well as flowers from as far away as New Zealand, Algeria and Chile. To learn more, go to *ubcbotanicalgarden.org* or call 604-822-9666.

A bounty of colors in Vail

Heckman rock garden in St. Louis

An anemone at Olbrich

ROCKY ROAD AHEAD. Whether you're dealing with rocky soil in Colorado, Missouri or even Wisconsin, these colorful and stunning gardens show just how much you can do with less-than-perfect conditions.

Great Lakes *paradise*

*Discover rare blooms at the wildflower sanctuary
near Green Bay, Wisconsin.*

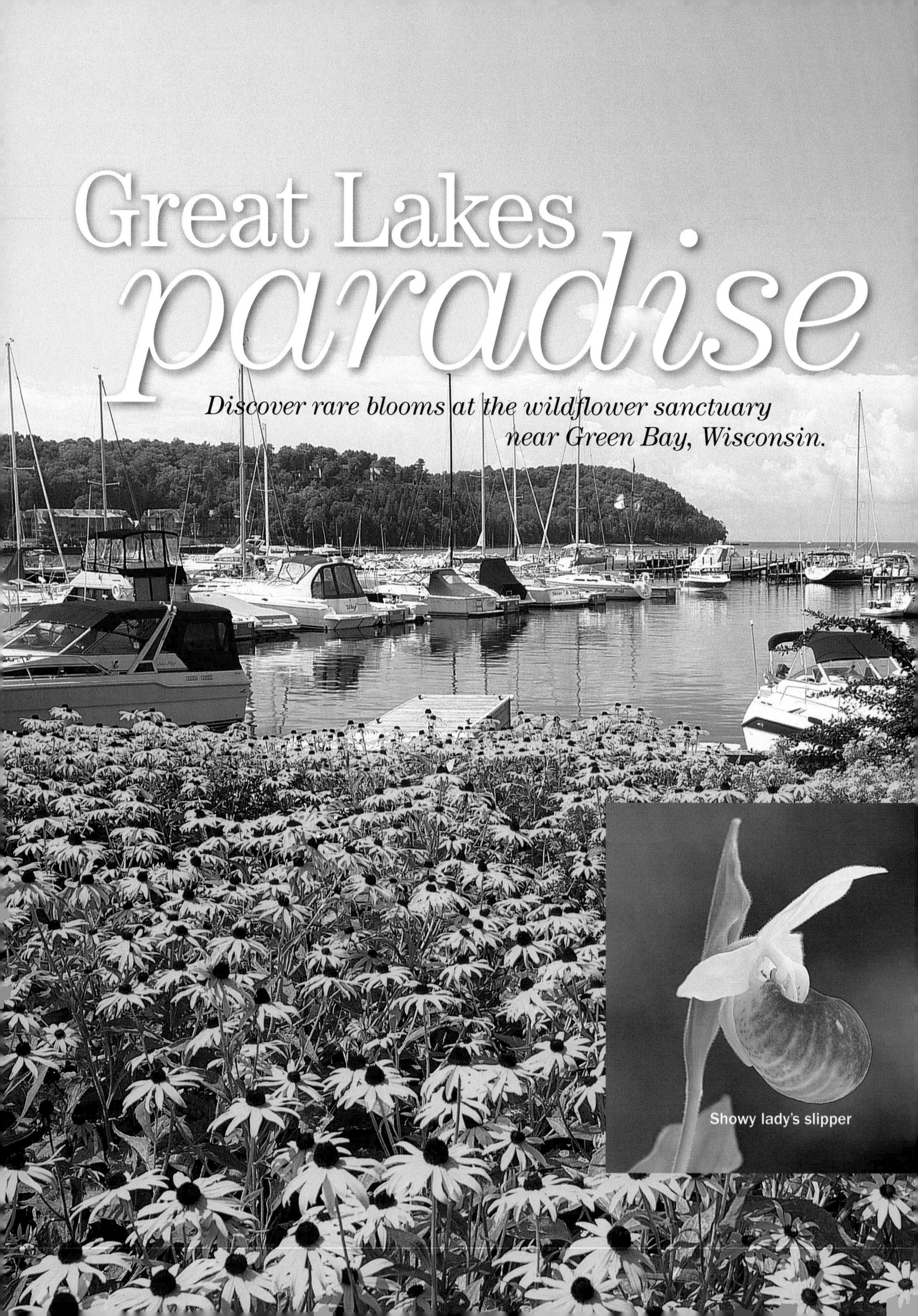

Showy lady's slipper

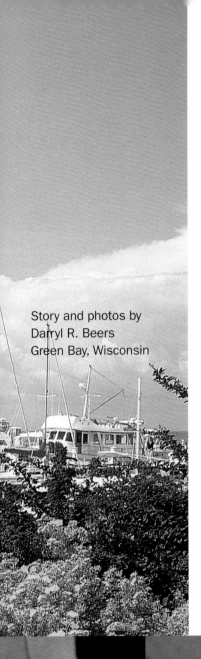

Story and photos by
Darryl R. Beers
Green Bay, Wisconsin

You never know where you will discover a hidden treasure. When I first set out with my photo gear to explore The Ridges Sanctuary along Wisconsin's Door Peninsula near Baileys Harbor, I didn't realize just how special this place was.

What I did know was that it was home to one of my favorite photo subjects, the threatened dwarf lake iris. In the entire world, this rare plant is known to grow only near the northern shores of Lake Michigan and Lake Huron.

Rounding a corner, I stopped dead in my tracks. I was in the midst of a sea of lavender-blue and green—the largest patch of dwarf lake irises I'd ever seen! For a nature photographer and wildlife aficionado, this place was nirvana.

The topography of The Ridges is the result of an evolutionary process. Lake Michigan water levels fluctuate in 30- to 50-year cycles. When the level is high, waves and currents push sand up on the beach to form ridges.

Star flower

Trout lily

Dwarf lake iris

Falling lake levels allow the ridges to grow and create marshy pools, called swales, between them. Over time, a series of 30 beach ridges and swales has been formed.

Southerly breezes over Lake Michigan make for a boreal, or Northwoods, climate at The Ridges. In conjunction with the ridges and swales, this climate contributes to the great diversity of plants growing in the area. More than 475 species of vascular plants live in the preserve. Of the 40 species of orchids found in Wisconsin, 25 inhabit The Ridges. In addition, at least 13 endangered or threatened species are denizens of this unique and fragile ecosystem.

The preserve was saved from development as a trailer park by a group of farsighted people who established The Ridges in 1937. The land owned and protected by the sanctuary has grown from a modest 40-acre tract to more than 1,600 acres.

In 1967, The Ridges became the first parcel of land in Wisconsin to be designated a National Natural Landmark. Membership in the sanctuary organization has grown to more than 3,300, representing 45 states and several foreign countries.

Each year, this distinctive wildflower preserve receives an estimated 25,000 visitors. Naturalists conduct guided nature tours every day from May through October, while you can take self-guided tours on the hiking trails anytime. Throughout the summer, the sanctuary offers many hands-on children's programs, as well as varied adult workshops and field trips.

The Ridges Sanctuary is indeed one of a kind. From the arctic primrose and trailing arbutus, which bloom in April, to the fringed gentian blossoms of autumn, this is a place of natural beauty, harmony and peace. It's a place with the power to rejuvenate the spirit and purify the soul— a special place created by nature and protected by humans.

For more information about The Ridges, visit *ridgessanctuary.org* or call 920-839-2802.

Shooting star

GO ON AN ADVENTURE. The Ridges Sanctuary has plenty of room for you to roam. At left, one of the foot bridges you'll find in the sanctuary. Above and on the next page, beautiful flowers line the pathways in and around the preserve in Door County.

Blue flag iris

Purple fringed orchid

Wood lily

Fringed gentian

Visit more wildflower sanctuaries in the Great Lakes states.

ELOISE BUTLER WILDFLOWER GARDEN AND BIRD SANCTUARY
Minneapolis, Minnesota

This 15-acre site is the oldest public wildflower garden in the nation, with more than 500 plant species in woodland, wetland and prairie habitats. It offers varied programs and classes throughout the spring and summer. Learn more at *minneapolisparks.org* or 612-370-4903.

DOWAGIAC WOODS NATURE SANCTUARY
Cass County, Michigan

This woodland sanctuary is renowned for its spring blossoms, with more than 50 wildflowers blooming in the spring. Easy, well-marked trails guide visitors through the 235-acre woods. Find more information at *michigannature.org* or 517-655-5655.

INDIAN BOUNDARY PRAIRIES
near Chicago, Illinois

Owned and protected by the Nature Conservancy, this 271-acre preserve consists of four prairies and is the largest remaining example of grassland prairie in Illinois. Designated a National Natural Landmark in 1988, it is home to many rare species, including the endangered prairie white fringed orchid, and a wealth of birds and butterflies. Find out more at *nature.org* or 866-876-5463.

KANKAKEE SANDS
Newton County, Indiana

Consisting of marsh wetlands, farm fields and prairie, this 7,800-acre preserve is an ongoing restoration project of the Nature Conservancy. To date, 5,000 acres have been restored with more than 390 native plant species. Friends of the Sands offer guided hikes and educational opportunities. Learn more at *nature.org* or 219-285-2184.

KITTY TODD NATURE PRESERVE
Lucas County, Ohio

As one of the finest preserves in the Oaks Openings region in Ohio, this 750-acre site is home to more than 100 state-listed rare plants. Guided walks and volunteer projects are available through the Nature Conservancy. Learn more at *nature.org* or 419-867-1521.

BOWMAN'S HILL WILDFLOWER PRESERVE
New Hope, Pennsylvania

Known as the state wildflower preserve of Pennsylvania, this 134-acre natural area features more than 800 native plant species. A visitor center welcomes guests and features intriguing exhibits, a library, a bird observatory and much more. You can even get married in the preserve's gazebo! For more information, visit *bhwp.org* or call 215-862-2924.

ALBANY PINE BUSH PRESERVE
Albany, New York

This 3,100-acre site encompasses one of the world's best remaining examples of an inland pine-barrens ecosystem. Featuring a hands-on environmental education facility called the Discovery Center, this state-owned preserve receives 100,000 visitors annually. Find out more at *albanypinebush.org* or 518-456-0655.

take your
pick

Pick-your-own flower farms offer a fun, inexpensive way to enjoy blooms.

By Stacy Tornio

WILDFLOWERS GALORE. Wildseed Farms in Texas is one of the best-known wildflower farms in the South. You can buy unique seeds, select your own flowers or even pick their famous chili peppers, $5 a bag.

Looking for a long-lasting arrangement? Choose blooms like yarrow, zinnias, sunflowers and gladioli for your vase. Yearning for something exceptionally beautiful and fragrant? David Austin roses last only a few days but are still worth it!

—**JUDY GARRY,** *Owner of Your Vase or Mine*

*W*hen I was a little girl, I could spend hours out in my parents' pasture as I searched for wildflowers to make the perfect bouquet. Now my two kids, ages 6 and 4, do the same thing. They meticulously hunt for blooms in our own garden, and then proudly present them to me when their collection is complete. Even though the arrangements are mostly thistle, dandelions and the like, I couldn't care less. My children's beaming smiles make it all worthwhile.

It doesn't matter how old you are: There's pride in being able to say you picked your own bouquet, especially when it comes from your own backyard. Unfortunately, wildflowers are often protected by state law, so you can't just go out and pick as you please. But now, thanks to all the flower farms popping up across the country, anyone can do this. Whether it's for an entire wedding party or just a single display, the pick-your-own phenomenon is giving flower lovers a new—and cheaper—way to enjoy their favorite blooms.

Growing a Business

When Judy Garry began gardening in 1996, she never dreamed strangers would one day be picking flowers from her own

Cutting Garden

Catherine's Fab Five

Catherine (above, with her husband, Tom, and dog, Salish) offers her top picks for vase flowers.

Sweet peas. A perfect accent flower.

Dahlias. Just the thing for late summer.

Asiatic lilies. Choose from dozens!

Peonies. Fabulous with aquilegia and lady's mantle.

Delphiniums. Tall and stately, they enhance any vase.

backyard. The Blue Ridge Mountains near her home in Asheville, North Carolina, must have provided some serious inspiration, though, because her gardens really started taking off. By 2005, she had more blossoms than she knew what to do with.

"I loved sharing my flowers with friends and neighbors, but the garden grew so big," Judy says. "I couldn't give them all away, so I decided to share my love and joy in flowers while making a little money to support my habit!"

After selling at a local market for a couple of years, Judy figured out it was easier to have people come directly to her. Today, at her business, Your Vase or Mine, customers make appointments to pick directly from her garden.

"Flowers can brighten up a room and make it come alive," she says. "They have such strong emotions attached to them. Flowers are nature's gift to us—pure beauty and joy."

Creating Memories

Catherine Mix has also made a business out of bouquets. Her flower farm in Sequim, Washington, hosts about 30 weddings each summer. The bridal flowers come from the pick-your-own area, which is open from dawn until dusk.

Even though Catherine has designed thousands of arrangements over the years, she still gets excited trying new color combinations. Fragrances inspire her, too.

"Our sense of smell is one of the strongest triggers for memories," she says. "Every year I close my eyes and deeply inhale the scents of each bloom in its season. The sweet smells remind me of other times and gardens—and I know that I'm making new memories about this time and place in my life, too."

I can relate to what Catherine says. From the Indian blankets I would collect as a young girl to the Shasta daisies my own children cut from our garden, the memories are always a little bit sweeter with flowers.

Top 10 Pick-Your-Owns From Around the Country

CUTTING GARDEN
SEQUIM, WASHINGTON

360-670-8671 ● *cuttinggarden.com*

This Washington hot spot is a favorite for many bridal parties. It makes a lovely location for weddings and receptions, providing stunning floral views both in the fields and on the tables. Open seven days a week from dawn to dusk, it's completely self-serve. A large bouquet is only $7.50.

FIELDS OF FLOWERS
PURCELLVILLE, VIRGINIA

540-338-7231 ● *fields-of-flowers.com*

Located near the Blue Ridge Mountains, this farm lets you pick Thursday through Saturday or by appointment until the first frost date. Prices are $10 for bouquets or $15 to $30 for buckets. For the latest in picking availability, contact the farm directly.

HELLERICK'S FAMILY FARM
DOYLESTOWN, PENNSYLVANIA

215-766-8388, *hellericksfarm.com*

You'll find plenty of flowers to choose from here, but what brings people in from afar are the famous zinnias. The large,

sturdy-stemmed beauties have been featured on TV and in magazines; you'll pay $3 a dozen. Open daily at 10 a.m. until they're sold out.

MELICK'S TOWN FARM
OLDWICK, NEW JERSEY

908-439-2318 ● *melickstownfarm.com*

You can buy a bouquet here, but it's a lot more fun to go out and select your own. Prices are per stem; after you've chosen your favorites, be sure to stroll around the farm, where you'll find baked goods, homemade jams and fresh fruits and veggies.

PARLEE FARMS
TYNGSBORO, MASSACHUSETTS

978-649-3854 ● *parleefarms.com*

You'll find more than 10 shades of Benary Giant zinnias to choose from, as well as sunflowers, gladioli and dahlias. After you pick a bouquet, they'll wrap them up for you to take home or give as a gift.

RIDGEFIELD FARM AND ORCHARD
HARPERS FERRY, WEST VIRGINIA

304-876-3647 ● *ridgefieldfarm.com*

According to the farm's website, a "reasonable bunch"

Your Vase or Mine

runs $7 to $15. The farm provides the scissors and hundreds of butterflies as you stroll through the garden. Picking runs from early July to mid-September.

SPRING LEDGE FARM
NEW LONDON, NEW HAMPSHIRE
603-526-6253 ● *springledgefarm.com*
Most people know Spring Ledge for its tasty you-pick strawberries, but it offers pick-your-own flowers as well. Prices run from around $12.50 a pound.

TAKE YOUR PICK FLOWER FARM
LANSING, NEW YORK
607-533-4680 ● *takeyourpickflowers.com*
At this self-service farm, you can stop by anytime between 9 a.m. and 7 p.m. and pick at will. Flowers are priced by the stem and range from 5 cents for lavender to 75 cents for sunflowers. Also check out the farm's Saturday booth at the Lansing Farmers Market.

WILDSEED FARMS
FREDERICKSBURG, TEXAS
800-848-0078 ● *wildseedfarms.com*
Buy some native wildflower seed, stop by the live butterfly exhibit or just enjoy the view at this Texas landmark. Look for the meadows area, which has been set aside especially for cutting flowers. They'll lend you a pair of scissors and a 32-ounce plastic cup with water to pick as many as you can fit inside. Call before you go to check the picking forecast. Late July brings the Chili Pepper and Salsa Festival; during and after the festival, pick fresh peppers for just $5 a bag well into August.

YOUR VASE OR MINE
ASHEVILLE, NORTH CAROLINA
828-299-4394 ● *yourvaseormine.com*
Judy Garry's gardens might not be as big as some, but they're big on color and selection. To arrange a time to pick your own, call or e-mail her (*yourvaseormine@charter.net*). Prices range from $20 for a single gallon bucket to $40 for 3 gallons, so grab a friend and save even more!

Wildseed Farms

traveling light

How to see the country's best botanical gardens for free. (No, really!)

Vacations can restore sanity. As a mother of three, I welcome every bit of time I get to spend with my husband and kids, but sometimes it's nice to get away from the carpooling and cooking and trade up to relaxation, fun and quality time.

By Amber Bruggman

Between everyday necessities and the little extras, it's hard to squeeze the budget just for the sake of family bonding. But help is on the way!

While pricey family attractions like amusement parks have their place, a great alternative is to reconnect with nature—and sometimes art—in a nearby setting. Public gardens are a great way to do this. And with just a little bit of planning, you can enjoy a relaxing day trip with your family without spending a dime.

Here are my top 10 "frugal mom" tips for making your next visit to a botanical garden your best and cheapest!

Do your research. While not all gardens are free, most offer free or

SUNKEN TREASURE. The sunken garden at Olbrich Botanical Gardens in Madison, Wisconsin, is a must-see. This free garden is one of the state's best. Left: The Missouri Botanical Garden in St. Louis is the country's oldest.

discounted days. Websites generally indicate who pays what and when.

Prepare for parking. Admission to the gardens may be free, but parking may cost you a bundle. Carpool with friends to save money, or research free parking options around the garden. You may end up walking a few blocks, but when parking can cost $20 or more, some exercise can keep a little of the green in your wallet.

Plan a "staycation." If you live in the same city or county as the garden, you might be eligible for free or reduced admission. Be sure to take proof of residence to get the discount.

Let your kids tag along. You might end up paying for yourself, but most gardens let children in free. And who knows? You could cultivate a real love of the outdoors when you expose your child to a wide range of beautiful flowers and plants.

Serve your country. While you might not join the military to get free garden admission, it can be one of the perks of service. Check it out if this applies to you.

Get a group together. Some gardens give group discounts, so while you won't exactly be getting in for free, you can save with friends and family outings.

Do good for others. Gardens sometimes offer discounted or free admissions when you bring canned goods or gently used clothing donations. Usually these perks are tied to local charitable organizations, so check with your food pantry or clothing drop-off location to see if something like this is offered.

Cheyenne Botanic Garden

Become a member. For a yearly fee, you get perks like free or reduced admission, free parking, and sometimes longer admission hours or access to special areas. Many gardens also allow free admission to other participating gardens with your membership.

Observe holidays. Many gardens stay open year-round, and a few offer free admission on certain holidays. For example, a garden might let you in free if you wear red on July Fourth. The garden's anniversary is also a popular time to offer reduced or free admission.

Set a budget. You may pay nothing for general admission, but special events and areas of the garden may not be free. Decide ahead of time which exhibits you want to visit, and make sure you're not tacking on hidden costs.

Take a closer look at these botanical gardens around the country to see how you might be able to get in free of charge!

BROOKLYN BOTANIC GARDEN • **Brooklyn, New York** • *bbg.org*
If you're in the mood for earth-friendly programs, stop by this world-famous garden, which holds more than 20 classes that are open to the public.
How to get in free: No admission charge Tuesdays or 10 a.m. to noon Saturdays. Seniors get in free on Fridays, too, and children and school groups are always free. More free admission: any weekday in the off-season, from Nov. 17 to March 2.

BIRMINGHAM BOTANICAL GARDENS • **Birmingham, Alabama** • *bbgardens.org*
Enjoy a wide variety of traditional and nontraditional gardens, including a Japanese garden with a teahouse and the wheelchair-accessible Enabling Garden.
How to get in free: Save your money for the gift shop. Admission and parking are free!

YERBA BUENA GARDENS • **San Francisco, California** • *yerbabuenagardens.com*
In addition to the flora, you'll see fascinating public art, including a glass ship sculpture that doubles as a greenhouse.
How to get in free: Go anytime. Enjoy waterfalls, meadows and more, all at no cost.

OLBRICH BOTANICAL GARDENS • **Madison, Wisconsin** • *olbrich.org*
Stop and smell the roses at this botanical garden. The rose area is a popular site and has been open to the public since 2005.
How to get in free: Admission is free, but some areas might have a nominal fee.

BELLEVUE BOTANICAL GARDEN • **Bellevue, Washington** • *bellevuebotanical.org*
Get your group a free guided tour of this garden just by contacting the staff. Free tours are also available on Saturdays and Sundays at 2 p.m.
How to get in free: Admission is free to all!

Bellevue Botanical Garden

Bellevue Botanical Garden

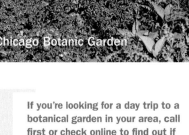

Chicago Botanic Garden

ZILKER BOTANICAL GARDEN • Austin, Texas • *zilkergarden.org*
Dinosaurs once roamed where the Cretaceous Garden grows. Along with plant
and insect life that existed 65 million years ago, a life-size dinosaur sculpture sits
on Dino Island.
How to get in free: General admission is free, though certain shows cost a bit extra.
Parking is free on weekdays and $3 per car on weekends.

CHEYENNE BOTANIC GARDENS • Cheyenne, Wyoming • *botanic.org*
This garden may not offer the largest acreage, but its focus on sustainability and
renewable energy makes it a must-see in the area. Even the Children's Village strives
to be eco-friendly, with recycled amphitheater seats and lessons in composting.
How to get in free: Just sign a guest book and enter at no cost.

ALASKA BOTANICAL GARDEN • Anchorage, Alaska • *alaskabg.org*
If you love the wild, this is the place for you. With the intent of keeping most of the
facility in a natural state, only 11 of its 110 acres are cultivated, so you never know
what you might spot while exploring the trails!
How to get in free: Become a member, or pay $5 to enter.

MISSOURI BOTANICAL GARDEN • St. Louis, Missouri • *mobot.org*
The land for the country's oldest botanical garden was a gift from Henry Shaw, whose
grand 1850 home stands here today.
How to get in free: Wednesdays and Saturdays before noon, there's no charge for resi-
dents of St. Louis County. Admission is also free to children and members, as is parking.

CHICAGO BOTANIC GARDEN • Glencoe, Illinois • *chicagobotanic.org*
Sitting on nine islands in the middle of a lake, this complex features formal gardens,
bird-watching areas, sculptures and more.
How to get in free: There's no admission charge, but parking is a steep $20 per car
and $25 per van. However, parking is just $7 for seniors on Tuesdays, and free for
members anytime.

If you're looking for a day trip to a botanical garden in your area, call first or check online to find out if there are daily deals or reduced admission fees.

a photographer's *dream*

North American birding trails make the perfect backdrop for nature photos.

Story and photos by Richard Cronberg

HITTING THE TRAIL. A path in Texas' Santa Ana National Wildlife Refuge welcomes birders. Photographers (inset) enjoy a day of shooting in Hagelstein Park near Klamath Lake, Oregon.

I'm not your typical tourist. When I go on vacation, I stay in places with few frills, arise and depart before dawn, and retire early each night. Birds are at the top of my agenda, so if it doesn't relate to nature, I generally don't have time to check it out.

Until recently, avid birders like me would travel great distances to famous birding destinations such as south Texas and go virtually unnoticed. But someone finally recognized the potential of catering to these atypical tourists!

A Nod to Birders

Texas officials were among the first to catch on. In 1996 the state's parks and wildlife department teamed up with local birders to develop a trail to mark birding locations. They numbered and mapped each site in a logical route. Finally, they began promoting their project as the Great Texas Coastal Birding Trail.

The plan quickly paid off as thousands of birders began following the trail and praising its virtues. Soon, merchants noticed a dramatic increase in business, and they started catering to birders.

It didn't take long for the word to get out. Florida began planning its own trail, and other states followed suit. Today, more than 35 states have one or more designated birding trails. Canada has joined in, too; there's a well-known trail in Saskatchewan, for instance.

Vermillion flycatcher

COASTAL BEAUTIES. One of the author's favorite trails is the Oregon Coast Birding Trail, where this photo was taken. It runs along the entire coast of Oregon, from Washington to California.

One of the best things about these trails is that they're easy to reach from paved roads. This is ideal for wildlife photographers. Not only do you not have to lug equipment as far, but the sites' popularity means that the birds are more tolerant of people, and therefore the birds are easier to photograph at close range.

Photography on the Trail

Photography is an important part of the trail system. Trail planners have made note of locations that have bird feeders, water features and photo blinds. Some trails even have nearby bed-and-breakfasts that cater to wildlife photographers and birders in general.

I've visited birding trails all over the country, including ones in Arizona, Florida and Texas. I also was one of the official photographers of the Oregon Coast Birding Trail, which covers the entire coastline from Washington into northern California, where you can find redwoods.

Although some think spring is the best season to visit these trails, many experienced birders enjoy summer and fall. Though most birds no longer sport breeding plumage, many species can be seen in abundance later in the year.

Fall is a great time to catch migratory species. In fact, if you're looking for something to do this fall, find out if the trails in your area have hawk-watching sites. These magnificent raptors steal the show this time of year.

Whether you're a seasoned photo pro or are just getting started, hit the road and check out the trails around you. Most have maps for purchase on-site and other helpful information for visiting.

Best Tips for Bird Photos on the Trail

- **Photograph in the best light of day.** Luckily, the best light occurs in early morning and late afternoon, when birds are most active anyway.

- **Use your car as a blind.** Many birds don't think of vehicles as a threat.

- **Focus on the eye.** If the eye of your subject isn't sharp, the photo doesn't look as good. Make the eye a priority.

- **Look for action.** A bird bathing, eating, stretching or preening is much more interesting than one perched on a stick.

- **Use a checklist.** Put together a checklist with the specifics for your camera so you'll be ready to shoot when the opportunity arises.

- **Anticipate action.** Most birds' motions can be predicted with a little observation. Being prepared will get you a better photo.

- **Use a tripod.** When it's possible, a tripod is definitely worthwhile. Blurry photos caused by camera movement can't be corrected.

- **Approach with caution.** When approaching birds, don't walk straight toward them or look directly at them. Meandering in a zigzag pattern and glancing at them only occasionally makes them feel less threatened.

Caspian tern

Redwoods along the
Oregon Coast Birding Trail

Green jay

Richard's Favorite State Trails

Southeastern Arizona Birding Trail, *seazbirdingtrail.com*

California Central Coast Birding Trail, *ca-ccbt.info*

The Great Florida Birding Trail, *floridabirdingtrail.com*

Birding Drives Dakota, *birdingdrives.com*

Oregon Coast Birding Trail, *oregoncoastbirding.com*

Great Texas Wildlife Trails, *tpwd.state.tx.us/huntwild/wild/ wildlife_trails/*

Tulips among blue forget-me-nots
Photo by Mark Turner

Tulips beneath a flowering crabapple tree
Photo by R. Todd Davis

Summer garden with cannas, cosmos and zinnias
Photo by Alan and Linda Detrick

Azalea in bloom in a rock garden
Photo by Judy White/Gardenphotos.

CHAPTER 7

Butterflies Galore

It's easy to attract butterflies to your backyard. All you need are the right plants, a little patience and a few secrets like these along the way.

Late Bloomers **180**

Containers: Attracting Butterflies **182**

Lend a Hand to Monarchs **184**

Beyond Butterflies **188**

Hosting Butterflies **192**

Lucky Seven **194**

Fritillary Welcome Mat **195**

Spring Beauties **196**

A Home for Hairstreaks **197**

Photos of the Year **198**

DONNA & TOM KRISCHAN

late bloomers

Grow late-season perennials to nourish southbound monarchs.

It's a win–win situation. You want late-season blooms to add color to your garden, and monarchs need good nectar sources to fuel their long journey to Mexico. To accomplish both tasks, consider adding late-flowering perennials and shrubs to your backyard. Favorites such as helianthus, eupatorium and asters attract nectar-seeking monarchs, as do late-flowering shrubs such as summersweet (*Clethera*) and blue mist spirea (*Caryopteris*).

One of the longest-blooming perennials is goldenrod, with its bright arching spires. This sun lover blooms from July until frost in Zones 3 to 9 and can reach 3 feet high and 3 feet wide. While its aggressive nature is usually best suited for wildflower areas, you can grow more compact cultivars, such as Fireworks, Little Lemon, Golden Fleece and Wichita Mountains, in your backyard.

Looking for more late-season fuel for orange and black beauties? Here are a few more all-star perennials that will attract hordes of hungry monarchs.

New England aster

Goldenrod

New England aster

Aster novae-angliae

Zones 4 to 8

This perennial grows to 6 feet high and 3 feet wide and bears clusters of deep-purple flowers with bright-yellow centers from August through October. Varieties are available in a range of colors from rose pink (as shown) to salmon, ruby red and purple. Plants prefer full sun and moist soil.

Turtlehead

Chelone glabra

Zones 3 to 8

Hooded white to pinkish-white blossoms resembling tiny turtle heads open in snapdragon fashion on leafy stems from August through October. Plants grow to 3 feet high and 2 feet wide and do best in partial shade and moist to wet enriched soil.

Turtlehead

New York ironweed

Vernonia noveboracensis

Zones 5 to 9

Ironweed produces clouds of purple blooms from August through September on sturdy, statuesque plants growing to 4 feet high and 3 feet wide. The adaptable, sun-loving perennial flourishes in any moist to normal soil.

New York ironweed

Meadow blazing star
Liatris ligulistylus
Zones 3 to 8
This clump-forming perennial produces puffs of rosy-purple flowers from July through September on plants growing to 3 feet high and 2 feet wide. The easy-grow plants require average well-drained soil and full sun.

containers
attracting butterflies

*Vibrant containers bring
beautiful winged creatures
to your backyard.*

It's always a joy to work in your garden and look up to see *butterflies fluttering overhead.*

Bee balm, verbena, lantana, butterfly bush and other plantings will invite angelic insects. The vivacious containers on these pages use flowers and bright colors that butterflies love.

Strong and Beautiful

These cute but hardy little pentas hold their own against heat and drought. Plant them in full sunlight in a 12-inch-diameter pot and watch the butterflies flock to them.

A Butterfly Red pentas (3)
B Glacier English ivy (1)
C Nicodemus plectranthus (1)

Pink Power

Brighten your day with this contrasting pink-and-white cluster in an 18-inch-diameter container. This mélange is full of plants and colors that will delight passing butterflies.

A Stratosphere™ Pink Picotee butterfly flower (Gaura) (1)
B Intensia® White phlox (1)
C Supertunia® Cotton Candy petunia (1)
D Wine & Roses® weigela (1)

Dynamic Duo

The butterflies won't be able to pry themselves away from this subtle yet elegant lantana. When you add a geranium to a 14-inch-diameter pot, the two pink flowers make a pretty pair.

A Landmark™ Rose Glow lantana (1)
B Showcase® Pink geranium (1)
C Blue Arrows juncus (1)

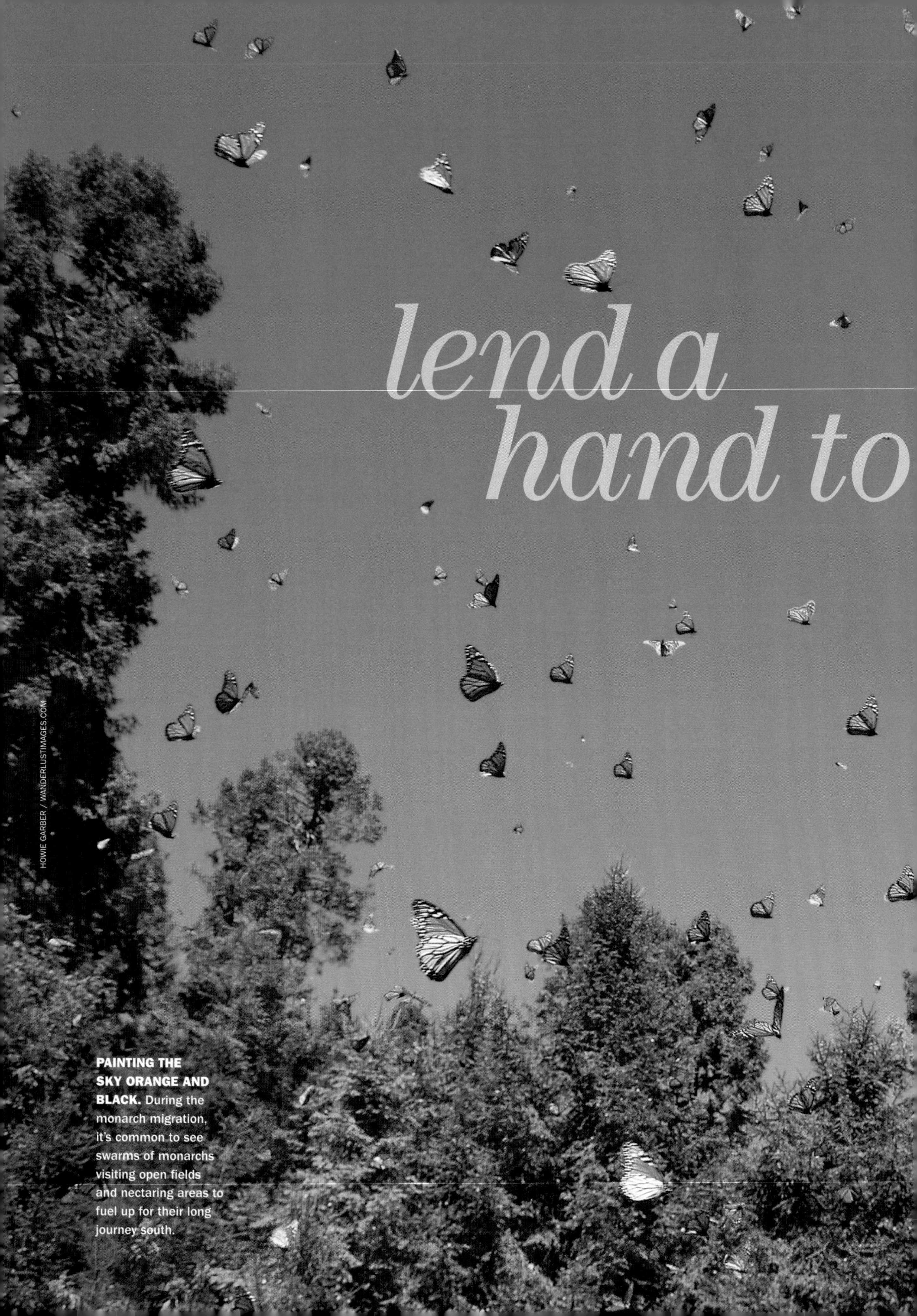

lend a hand to

PAINTING THE SKY ORANGE AND BLACK. During the monarch migration, it's common to see swarms of monarchs visiting open fields and nectaring areas to fuel up for their long journey south.

HOWIE GARBER / WANDERLUSTIMAGES.COM

monarchs

Help a migrating monarch by preserving its territory.

By Crystal Rennicke

It's one of the great mysteries of nature. Each fall, hundreds of millions of monarchs throughout the United States and Canada migrate to central Mexico for the winter, some traveling up to 3,000 miles. These miraculous fliers live less than 12 months and make the trip only once, yet somehow find their way back to the same fir-tree forests where previous generations have wintered for years.

The wintering grounds of these butterflies are a remarkable sight—swarms of monarchs fill the trees and the hum of flapping wings is deafening. Unfortunately, over the years, weather catastrophes and the deforestation of these grounds have taken a toll. Some statistics report a 50 to 80 percent decline over the years. And the World Wildlife Fund has listed the monarch migration as an endangered phenomenon. Despite all this, there are ways to help these amazing fliers.

The Fight for Land

In order to make a big comeback, it's really a matter of math. Monarchs need to increase their numbers up here in the north.

"The monarch's ability to repopulate is determined by the amount of habitat left in the United States," says Barb Agnew, founder of the Monarch Trail in southeast Wisconsin. "Every day we lose 6,000 acres of land across the country. Developers like flat, open fields—exactly the habitat required by most butterfly species, including the monarch."

For Barb, this hits close to home. For four years she has dedicated her time and energy to protecting one of these essential butterfly way stations on 89 acres dubbed the Monarch Trail, located in an urban area of Milwaukee. But now the

TO DEFEND AND PROTECT. Standing among several milkweed plants along the Monarch Trail in Milwaukee, Barb Agnew proudly defends this urban acreage for migrating monarchs.

RESTING PLACE. A group of monarchs stopped at the Monarch Trail in Milwaukee while headed to their winter grounds.

how to help

If you're looking for a way to help, check to see if there are any **local organizations** dedicated to preserving an area near you. Also, try looking to larger organizations like **Monarch Watch** (*monarchwatch.org*) that help to educate the public about monarch migration and encourage people to create habitats in home gardens, school properties, businesses and other plots of land.

Finally, never underestimate the importance of your own backyard. Even if you can't preserve a vast field for monarchs, you can help on a smaller scale. Try **planting a butterfly garden**, complete with milkweed and other nectar plants.

city is looking to develop the site.

"The Monarch Trail was established because I needed people to witness the migration in order to convince them that this area must be preserved," says Barb. "Monarchs need this rest area to fuel up for their long journey south in fall. It also serves as an essential roosting site for future generations."

Barb and the supporters of the Monarch Trail have written letters and attended meetings to try to save it. While a good portion of the land will still be developed, the group did manage to get a slice of it designated just for monarchs. It was a small victory, but a big moment for Barb.

The Big Picture

Barb's story is all too familiar. Across America, month after month, important monarch habitats are lost to land development. In the past 16 years, some 35 million acres have been destroyed, an area about the size of Illinois.

Of course, many gardeners do their part by planting milkweed, a monarch's host plant and its caterpillars' sole food source. But the bigger task is to preserve large parcels of land.

"Vast open areas that once supported large populations cannot be replicated in our gardens," says Barb. "Many butterflies need specific features like wetlands and require host plants that most people don't want in their yards."

For example, the red admiral butterfly and tortoiseshell caterpillars feed on stinging nettle. Dill is host to black swallowtails, and pearly everlasting plants play host to American lady butterflies. These wild, weedy plants aren't exactly backyard favorites. This is why public land is so important, Barb reiterates. And it's why so many people are fighting for areas like the Monarch Trail every day.

"Communities can be successful in preserving some of the natural fields and open areas for various bird and butterfly species," Barb says. "I believe that if the numbers rise and the land is restored, this migratory path will continue to provide a glimpse of a much larger international phenomenon."

beyond butterflies

Put out the welcome mat for these beneficial insects.

Story and photos by Bill Johnson
Minneapolis, Minnesota

When we think of beneficial insects in the garden, butterflies are usually at the top of the list. However, if we could take a bug census, we would discover that butterflies make up one of the smallest percentages of all insects visiting our gardens.

From dragonflies to bees, hundreds of insects frequent our backyards. And while a small handful are considered pests, most are beneficial or are completely harmless.

In my own backyard, we leave a small part of our lawn wild to create a natural habitat for our insect visitors. In turn, we attract a wide variety of crawlers, fliers and hoppers that pollinate our flowers, gather nectar and eat pesky bugs. In addition, they enhance the garden experience with their beautiful colors or sounds.

While specific insects vary greatly by region, here are a few that you actually want to see in your yard this spring and summer. Go ahead and take a closer look outside. You just might be amazed at what you find.

Widow skimmer

Twelve-spotted skimmer

dragonflies

Twelve-spotted skimmer (*Libellula pulchella,* wingspan 3 inches)
You'll notice these dragonflies throughout the summer, flying over gardens look-ing for food. Because they—and all dragonflies—have multifaceted eyes, they are extremely good hunters and eat all sorts of insects, especially mosquitoes.

Green darner dragonfly (*Anax junius,* wingspan 4+ inches)
These are our largest dragonflies. Very strong fliers and commonly seen, they're one of the best insect-eaters in our gardens. Green darners start their lives as nymphs in water and emerge as winged adults. Nymphs eat mosquito larvae, and the adults eat the mosquitoes that bite us.

Widow skimmer dragonfly (*Libellula luctuosa,* wingspan 3 inches)
You can often spot this common dragonfly perched upon the tip of a stick or branch, staking out a territory for hunting. They will chase off other dragonflies. They eat mosquitoes and many other insects. The white patches on the wings and the pale blue abdomen identify this one as a male. The female has no white on her wings, and her abdomen is brown with orange stripes on the sides.

Widow skimmer dragonfly

Green darner dragonfly

beetles

Milkweed leaf beetle

Milkweed leaf beetle (*Labidomera clivicollis*, ⅜ inch)

This distinctly colored beetle is common in gardens where milkweed has been allowed to grow. Often mistaken for ladybugs, they're almost twice the size of the common ladybug.

Pennsylvania leatherwing beetle

Pennsylvania leatherwing beetle
(*Chauliognathus pennsylvanicus*, ⅝ inch)

Common in gardens and considered beneficial, these beetles transfer pollen from flower to flower, plus they eat aphids and other insect pests. If you have goldenrod or Joe Pye weed in your garden, you'll very likely see them on those plants.

Red milkweed beetle

Red milkweed beetle (*Tetraopes tetrophthalmus*, ½ inch)

If there are any milkweeds in your garden, this beetle will show up, especially if you grow common milkweed, its favorite host plant. Its bright red color warns birds and other insects, "Don't eat me. I'm toxic."

bees

Bumble bee

Honeybee (*Apis mellifera*, ⅝ inch)

Besides being the producers of the honey that we eat, honeybees serve as major pollinators of flowers and crops. They're known as social insects because they live in large colonies. Although they're capable of stinging, they will do so only when they feel threatened.

Bumble bee (*Bombus* species, ¾ inch)

One of the most entertaining insects in the garden, it's a rather clumsy flier and stays on flowers such as monarda and coneflowers long enough for you to take a picture. You can see the pollen sacs on its hind legs. A very beneficial pollinator, it is capable of stinging, but will do so only if it thinks you plan to harm it.

Virescent green metallic bee (*Agapostemon virescens*, ½ inch)

You'll see this bee in most gardens. A shiny green metallic head and thorax and banded abdomen clearly make it stand out from other bees and wasps. This bee, which is a pollinator, makes its nest in the ground.

Virescent green metallic bee

Honeybee

Bee fly

flies

Bee fly (*Poecilanthrax* species, ½ inch)
This flier gets its name because it resembles a furry bee. What looks like a
stinger going into the flower is actually a proboscis (tongue) it uses to gather
nectar. It's harmless, can't sting and serves as a beneficial pollinator.

Long-legged fly

Long-legged fly (*Condylostylus* species, ¼ inch)
These very common flies can be seen racing around on leaves. They eat aphids,
mites and other small insects. Their metallic colors—in bronze, blue, green or
gold—make them easy to see when sunlight hits them.

Flower fly

Flower fly (*Helophilus fasciatus*, ⅝ inch)
These flies help control aphids, especially their larvae. They also pollinate by
flying from flower to flower. As part of their self-defense, several species are
considered very good bee mimics with coloration that looks quite similar to
bees. But because they're flies, they don't have the ability to sting.

other beneficial bugs

Broad-winged katydid (*Microcentrum rhombifolium*, 2 inches)
Katydids are a common sight at night near light sources. The night calls of the
adults are part of the evening symphony throughout the summer into fall.

Green lacewing

Green lacewing (*Chrysopa* species, ½ inch)
This beautiful insect is very common and very beneficial. Its larvae eat as many
aphids as they can find. You'll see it during the day throughout the garden and
at night near light sources.

Snowy tree cricket (*Oecanthus fultoni*, ¾ inch)
You probably haven't seen these, but you've definitely heard them. In late
summer and into the fall, the chirping you hear in the evening comes from
snowy tree crickets. They're not very big, but they can make an amazing
amount of noise.

Monarch on asters

hosting butterflies

Include host plants in your garden to keep 'em coming back for more.   By Tom Allen

Flowers vs. host plants. Which do you choose?

On one hand, flowers attract butterflies to your backyard because they are a reliable nectar source. (And they're pretty!) On the other hand, it's the host plants that keep them coming back because they offer a place for adults to lay their eggs.

The good news is: You don't have to choose! A successful butterfly garden offers both nectar and host sources. And you can even find a few plants that provide both.

Take milkweed, for example. Not only is it a good nectar source for butterflies, it's also the sole host plant for monarchs.

To help strengthen your butterfly garden, I put together this Top 10 list of host plants. Species will vary by region, so you might want to check with your local garden expert. But for the most part, these trees, shrubs, grasses and flowers do well throughout the country.

1. Willows. Many trees serve as hosts for butterflies, but willows are one of the most popular. My favorite is the weeping willow, which makes a nice ornamental. Host to: Mourning cloaks, Compton's tortoise-shells, viceroys, admirals, duskywing skippers, western tiger swallowtails and a few sulphurs.

2. Oaks. In Northern areas, young white oaks are a favorite for hair-streaks and skippers, but in the South, live oaks are more popular. Many of the hairstreaks that use oaks lay their eggs in the bud axils of the follow-ing spring's new growth. Caterpil-lars hatch along with the new leaf growth. Host to: Several hairstreak butterflies and duskywing skippers.

3. Wild cherry. Young admiral caterpillars overwinter in a rolled-up leaf attached to a wild cherry tree by silk. Then they feed on the tree's new growth in spring. The blues and hairstreaks lay their eggs on the flower buds, and the caterpillars feed on the flowers and the fruit in springtime. Host to: Coral and striped hairstreaks, red-spotted purples, white admirals in the north, spring azure blues, and eastern, Canadian and western tiger swallowtails.

4. New Jersey tea. This small, evergreen shrub serves well as a host plant and has white flowers that produce an abundance of nectar. Host to: Mottled duskywings, spring azure blues and brown elfins in the East. In the West, similar shrubs in the Ceanothus family are used by Arizona and hedgerow hairstreaks, Percuvius duskywings and California tortoiseshells.

5. Grasses. Of the herbaceous plants used as hosts, probably the most widely used group is grasses. For best results, look up the grasses in your area that skippers prefer. Host to: Wood nymphs, satyrs, arctics and skippers.

6. Asters. Aster varieties vary a great deal by area, but New England asters are attractive additions to almost any North American garden. They're also an excellent nectar source for those late-season butterflies, including migrating monarchs. Host to: Crescents (tawny, northern, field and pearl) and checkerspots (Hoffman's, northern and silvery).

7. Violets. Fritillaries seek out plants in this popular family to lay their eggs. Many violets, including Johnny-jump-ups and pansies, are shade-tolerant plants, so you can plant them under or near other good

Red clover

RICHARD SHIELL

nectar sources to increase the traffic to your garden. Host to: Most fritillaries in the U.S.

8. Legumes. It's best to do a little research when it comes to the legume family. Wisteria, clovers, various sennas and garden beans are all legumes that attract a variety of butterflies. Check with a good source in your area for advice on what you can attract locally. Host to: Many of the open-winged skippers, as well as several blues and sulphurs.

9. Mallows. Mallows attract lots of butterflies and are also excellent host plants. Hollyhocks, which are among the tallest plants in this family, make wonderful hosts, but don't stop there. Check with a local garden source for good mallow recommendations. Host to: Checkered and powdered skippers, hairstreaks (gray, mallow scrub and red-crescent scrub) and west coast ladies.

10. Mustards. Many species of butterflies use mustards as host plants. Plants in this family include broccoli, cabbage and their relatives. Another popular plant in this family is nasturtiums. Host to: Several whites and marbles, and falcate and sara orangetips.

Willow

GRAHAM RICE / GARDENPHOTOS.COM

Cabbage white

RICK & NORA BOWERS / KAC PRODUCTIONS

Hollyhocks

WILLIAM H. JOHNSON

PLANTS WITH A PURPOSE. When choosing new trees, shrubs or flowers for your yard, be sure to select plants that appeal to butterflies as well. For instance, hollyhocks (above) are a host plant to both skippers and hairstreaks.

Monarch on butterfly bush

JOE PYE WEED: MONARCH ON BUTTERFLY BUSH: ANN GORDON

lucky *seven*

These perennials are a must when it comes to attracting butterflies. By Tom Allen

A good butterfly garden has a wide array of perennial blooms with an abundance of nectar sources. But when it comes to the best of the best, it's hard to narrow it down.

Here are my top seven suggestions for must-have backyard butterfly plants. If you're just getting started or have only a small space, these are the ones to go to first. If you're a more seasoned gardener, these are the staples you can never have enough of!

Milkweed. Tall and short milkweeds will highlight any garden with colors ranging from white and pink to deep orange. Because milkweed is the monarch's host plant, it serves a dual purpose, providing high-quality nectar as well as food for the caterpillars.

New York ironweed. This North American native grows well, offering large clumps of purple flowers that attract skippers as well as larger butterflies.

Butterfly bush. This buddleja species has a small-flowered cluster of blooms on a woody shrub that is sought after by most butterflies. It attracts fliers of all sizes, especially summer fritillaries, and comes in a variety of colors. Be aware that it is invasive in some areas. Try Lo & Behold Blue Chip, a smaller, noninvasive cultivar.

Joe Pye weed. This tall, flowering plant has deep-pink flowers that thrive in either wet or dry sites with full sunlight. Fritillaries love it!

Hollyhocks. These tall beauties serve as both host plants and nectar sources for several butterfly species. If you have just a small space, you should include these climbers.

Coneflowers. They add wonderful color and are a dependable nectar source for almost any perennial bed.

Asters. Every garden should have perennial asters. Their rich fall color is perfect for late-season sulphurs and migrating monarchs. The New England aster is my personal favorite.

Joe Pye weed

fritillary
welcome mat

Bring these beauties to your yard with a few simple plants!

Gardening for butterflies isn't difficult. You just have to offer the right kind of plants.

For example, fritillaries use the violet family (*Viola*) as host plants. This means the butterflies will lay their eggs only on violet plants because their caterpillars need them to survive. Take the great spangled fritillary, pictured at right. Its caterpillar, which is black with orange spines, hibernates in winter. As soon as it emerges, it feeds on violet leaves in early spring.

Planting native wild violets is always a plus for any butterfly garden, but it doesn't mean it's the only plant that will attract fritillaries. From host plants to nectar sources, here are a few favorites to lure these fliers into your garden.

Johnny-jump-up
Host Plant
(*Viola tricolor*, annual)
This popular annual has small flowers from spring to autumn in shades of purple, lavender-blue, white or yellow. While the blooms tend to be short-lived, they readily self-seed.

Butterfly bush
Host Plant
(*Buddleja davidii*, Zones 5 to 9)
Although invasive in some states, this avid bloomer is beneficial to butterfly gardens. Fritillary butterflies will flock to this plant for a sweet treat.

Pansy
Host Plant
(*Viola* x *wittrockiana*, annual)
You can find pansies in nearly any shade. Grown as annuals in most areas, they flower in spring and through fall. Newer cultivars even offer winter and early spring flowering.

Purple coneflower
Nectar Plant
(*Echinacea*, Zones 3 to 9)
These beauties are like a magnet to butterflies. They offer a long-lasting nectar source from midsummer to early fall.

Purple coneflower

Johnny-jump-up

Butterfly bush

Milbert's tortoiseshell. You can find this one in Northern and Western states; look for its striking patterns of dark brown against broad bands of yellow and orange. This flier is a colonial hibernating species, beginning to emerge in spring as soon as the snow melts. It uses nettles as host plants.

Red admiral. This is a dark-chocolate brushfoot butterfly (left) with an unmistakable bright red-orange band across its wings and white spots on black at the wingtips. Red admirals winter in the South and migrate northward in search of host plants, including nettles, as spring approaches.

Malachite. This tropical flier is a jewel of southern Florida and Texas. While it doesn't have a huge range, its beautiful lime-green pattern on chocolate brown makes it one of the easiest-to-distinguish fliers in North America. The malachite readily feeds at flowers and on rotting fruit. In Florida, you'll find its caterpillar on green shrimp plants; else-where, it seeks out plants in the acanthus family.

spring
beauties

Here are five of the most colorful spring butterflies around. By Tom Allen

Spring is bursting with color from the flowers in your backyard, but if you take a closer look you might notice some butterflies among those blooms. These five fliers are some of the earliest and most beautiful around. Learn where to spot them and how to attract them to your backyard today.

Zebra swallowtail. This large butterfly (top) has zebra stripes and a red spot at the base of its hindwings. Since it emerges from an overwintering pupa,

it's one of the earliest fliers throughout much of the eastern United States. Look for this beauty along wooded habitats and streams and wherever its host plant, pawpaw, grows.

Sara orangetip. You can find this delicate butterfly (right) along foothills, canyons and streams throughout the West. This flier is usually white or pale yellow, with red-orange and black wing tips. To attract this orangetip, offer host plants like mustard or rock cresses.

A *Home for* Hairstreaks

Attract these fliers with easy-grow native plants.

RICK & NORA BOWERS / KAC PRODUCTIONS

If you want to draw this white-banded beauty into your yard, cultivate fruit-bearing shrubs and trees that nourish its caterpillars and summer-blooming plants that supply nectar to adult butterflies.

Striped hairstreak butterflies lay their eggs, which hatch the following spring, on all sorts of host plants that provide food for their larvae. They flock to landscapes where raspberries, dewberries and blackberries (Rubus), apples (Malus pumilia), cherries (Prunus), pears (Pyrus), American hornbeams (Carpinus caroliniana), paper birches (Betula papyrifera) and hickories (Carya) flourish. In addition to these favored host plants, many other garden-worthy plants will beautify your mixed borders while turning them into hairstreak hot spots. Here's a look at just a few:

Northern highbush blueberry

JUDYWHITE / GARDENPHOTOS.COM

Common milkweed

ROLAND JORDAHL

Northland highbush blueberry
Host Plant
(*Vaccinium corymbosum* 'Northland', Zones 3 to 8)
Producing bell-shaped white flowers in May and plump, flavorful fruits in summer, this 4-by-4-foot bush supplies food for butterfly larvae, butterflies, birds, small mammals and humans. This is a plant for all seasons: Green leaves shift to orange in autumn, and the red stems are pretty through winter.

Common milkweed
Nectar Plant
(*Asclepias syriaca*, Zones 3 to 9)
Best known as the host of monarch butterflies, this native (and naturalizing) milkweed draws in all types of butterflies. Plants growing to 4 feet high and 1 foot wide produce showy, fragrant clusters of pinkish-white flowers from June to August.

Common chokecherry
Host Plant
(*Prunus virginiana*, Zones 2 to 7)
Ideally suited for forming protective thickets for both birds and butterflies, chokecherry grows to 20 to 30 feet high and wide. It produces clusters of scented white flowers in spring and red berries that deepen to purple by late summer. Try the popular purple-leafed cultivar Shubert Select (also called Canada Red) to bring butterflies and unexpected foliage color to backyard vistas.

Common chokecherry

JUDYWHITE / GARDENPHOTOS.COM

New Jersey tea
Nectar Plant
(*Ceanothus americanus*, Zones 4 to 8)
Low-growing shrubs, growing to 3 feet high and 5 feet wide, supply shelter and nectar for visiting butterflies. Sweet-smelling 2-inch panicles of small white flowers bloom from June into August.

New Jersey tea

DONNA & TOM KRISCHAN

Regal moth on rudbeckia
Photo by Richard Day / Daybreak Imagery

Anise swallowtail
Photo by Richard Shiell

Luna moth
Photo by Nancy Rotenberg

Cabbage white on salvia
Photo by Bill Leaman / Positive Images

Monarch
Photo by James Cihula

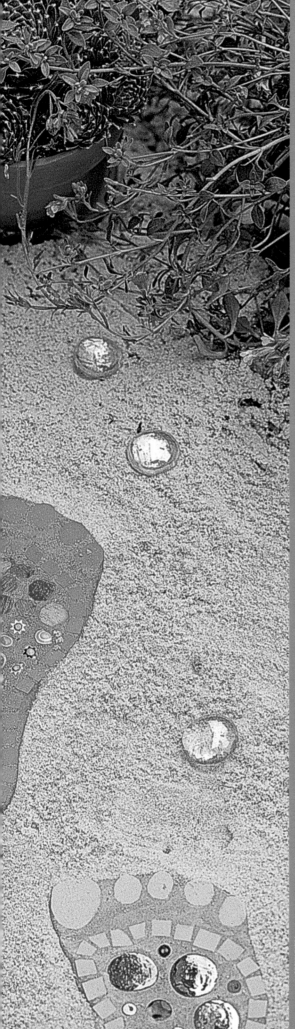

BECKY PATON

CHAPTER 8

DIY Backyard

Save money and get an "I-did-it-myself" satisfaction with the projects and ideas on the following pages. They're easy with our step-by-step instructions—and your backyard will be filled with fun projects!

Junkyard Creations **202**

5-Minute Feeder **209**

Music in the Garden **210**

Green-Roof Birdhouse **212**

Upcycled Bird Feeder **214**

Footprints in the Sand **216**

Silverware Suet Feeder **218**

Break the Mold **220**

junkyard

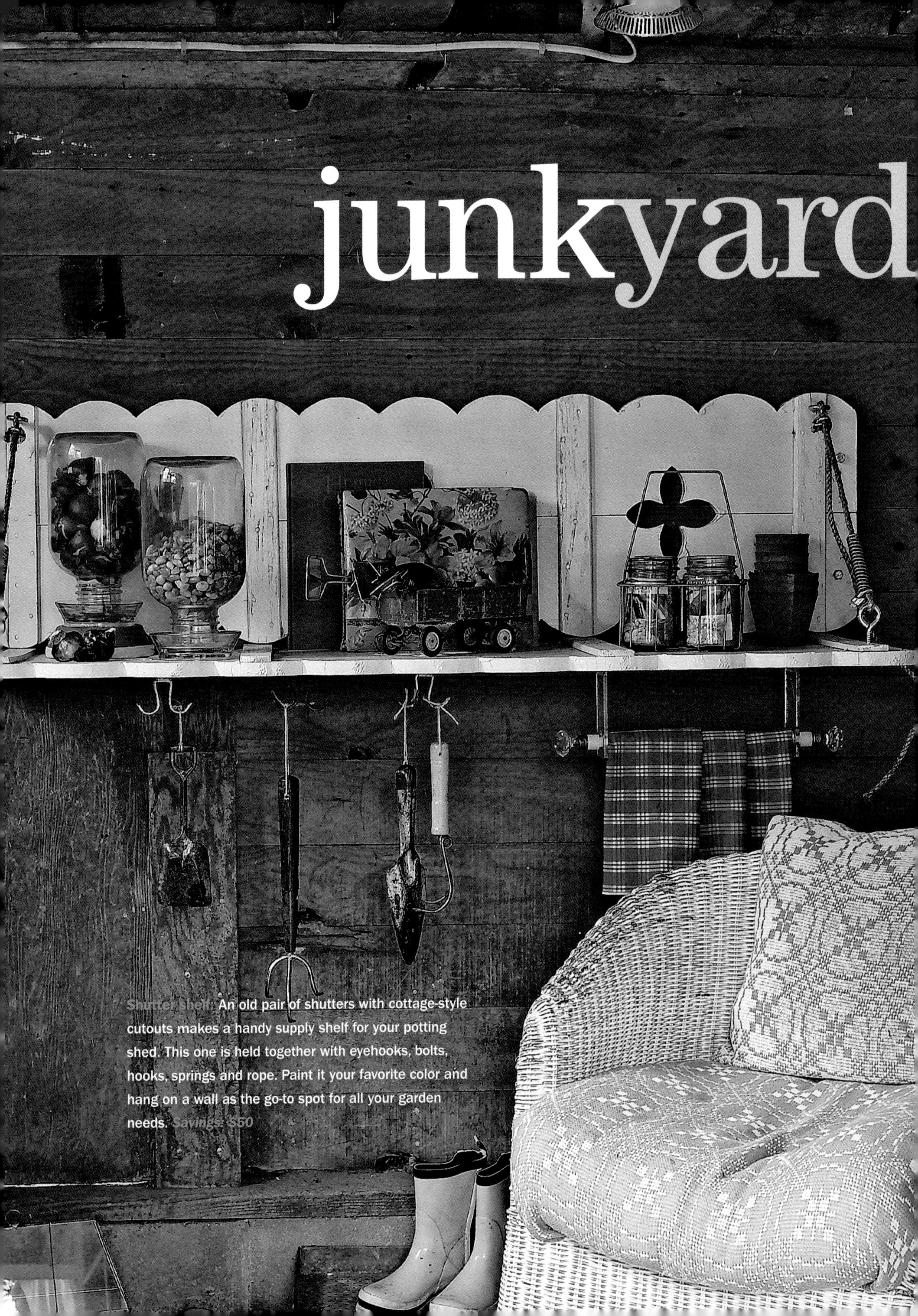

Shutter Shelf An old pair of shutters with cottage-style cutouts makes a handy supply shelf for your potting shed. This one is held together with eyehooks, bolts, hooks, springs and rope. Paint it your favorite color and hang on a wall as the go-to spot for all your garden needs. **Savings: $50**

creations

These "junkers" show that with a little imagination and an eye for finding treasures in the trash, you can outfit your yard for free!

By Crystal Rennicke

As the trend of doing more with less continues to grow, what better option than to decorate your outdoor spaces with some creatively deployed junk?

This idea gallery—excerpted from the book *Junk Beautiful: Outdoor Edition,* by Sue Whitney of *junkmarketstyle.com* and designer Kim Melamed—will have you well on your way to repurposing your trash and rethinking outdoor decor. All you need are an open mind and a little time to discover what treasures lie in your trash. Then you can use the inspiration gleaned from these pages to create your own backyard paradise.

Chic candleholder: Greet your guests with a warm glow from this candleholder placed at an entryway or pathway. Look closely—it's actually the inner workings of an old electric heater with a pillar candle inside! *Savings: $40*

Twice-as-nice tools: Put old tools back to work as garden art. Attach old chisels or other tools with rope to a vintage strainer for a one-of-a-kind wind chime. *Savings: $35*

Teapot planter: Adorn an old enameled teapot with some vintage salt spoons and add funky drawer knobs to the bottom. Create a few holes for a little drainage, and you've got a pretty place to pot your flowers. *Savings: $20*

Have you accumulated a collection of mismatched vintage drawer knobs? Be creative in how you reuse them. They could make smart accessories for birdhouses, containers and garden art.

Galvanized vase covers: Gussy up plain-Jane vases by slipping these metal covers over them. These were crafted from galvanized corrugated tin (you can use new tin from the hardware store, too), bolts, wing nuts and washers. *Savings: $25*

Thrifty torchlight: Instead of tiki torches, try shedding light on your backyard with an apple picker affixed to an old rake handle. Set a glass bowl with a candle inside to cast an inviting glow. *Savings: $30*

Seed caddy: Store and tote your seeds with ease using this simple caddy made of mason jars. To see what you've got, line each jar with the corresponding seed packet. *Savings: $15*

Budget beverage station: Entertaining outdoors? This drink station is made from an old restaurant wash-and-dry station. The sinks serve as ice buckets, while the drying area holds your glasses and utensils. *Savings: $150*

Planter with panache: Hang this planter from a doorway for a conversation piece to welcome your guests. It's made from half an old drawer, a frame and some vintage letters and numbers. *Savings: $25*

Kid-friendly picnic table: Make a fun kid's table out of an old wagon. Complete the table setting with kid Adirondack chairs, enamelware dishes and metal cups for little diners. *Savings: $25*

make this yourself! NEXT PAGE

wagon picnic table

This little red wagon is a perfect tabletop for your pint-sized guests.

Instructions

1. With a screwdriver, remove the bases from the folding tables.

2. Clean the tabletops with Wood-finish Cleaner (Photo A).

3. Place the hinges on the ends of the wagon and tabletops and mark the holes. You want the hinges on the ends so the top opens in the center of the wagon.

4. Drill the marked locations. It may be helpful to remove the tops and end pieces of the wagon to do this.

5. Attach the hinges with the screws and nuts using pliers (Photo B).

6. Once both the tabletops are secured, lay out the lock hardware on the center where the tables meet and attach the lock mechanism using a screwdriver (Photo C).

What You Will Need

- Vintage child's wagon
- 2 old wooden folding tables
- 4 hinges
- Screws and nuts (they may come with the hinges)
- Slide-bolt lock set
- Skidmore's Woodfinish Cleaner
- Screwdriver
- Drill
- Needle-nose pliers

For more inspiration on outdoor decor on a budget, pick up a copy of *Junk Beautiful: Outdoor Edition* (Taunton Press, $21.95).

5-minute feeder

Orioles will flock to this feeder filled with grape jelly or sugar water.

By Dottie Baltz

You don't have to do a lot of work to attract orioles. These bright orange fliers will gladly come to your backyard for sugar water, jelly or fruit. Here's a simple project that is perfect for gauging the oriole interest in your area. You can do it in less than five minutes, and when you use recycled items, it'll cost only a couple of bucks at most.

Instructions

1. Using the needle-nose pliers, make a small hook at one end of the 10-gauge wire. This will be the feeder's hanger.
2. Starting at the hanger end, gently bend the wire into an arch. You can use a round object to help with this or you can bend it freehand.
3. Approximately 12 in. from the hanger end, bend the wire at about a 45-degree angle. Place the shot glass on top of the wire and bend the wire around the bottom.
4. Cup the wire and glass in one hand while wrapping most of the remaining wire tightly around the glass.
5. At this point, you should have about 6 to 8 in. of wire remaining. Curve it into a "C" shape in front of the glass to make a perch.
6. To help the feeder hang better, gently twist the main part of the hanger a quarter turn to the right or left.
7. Next, to decorate, take the 18-gauge copper wire and start wrapping it around the 10-gauge wire near the top of the hanger.
8. Wrap the last few inches of wire around a pen to make a curlicue.
9. Attach beads in alternating sizes. To secure the beads, curl the end of the wire with needle-nose pliers.

What You Will Need

- 3 ft. 10-gauge copper wire
- 12 in. 18-gauge copper wire
- Double shot glass (3 oz.)
- Wire strippers or cutters
- Needle-nose pliers
- Pen
- Glass beads

To see more of Elsa's
beautiful beaded work
or to buy one of her
unique wind chimes,
visit her website at
tempestinateapot.net.

Music in the garden

Relax with the soothing sounds of this wind chime made from an old teapot, silverware and beads. By Elsa Mikus

Lounge around on a breezy day listening to the sweet sounds of this artistic wind chime. It helps to have a little experience in beading to make the strands, but even if you don't, it's easy to figure out once you get going. For this design, we used a vintage teapot, but you can also use an old sugar bowl, gravy boat or other dining accessory. Let your imagination lead the way!

Instructions

1. Search your local flea markets and secondhand stores (or even your attic) for a vintage silver teapot and silver-plated flatware.

What You Will Need

- Vintage teapot
- Silver-plated flatware, 5 pieces
- Formula 409 cleaner
- Black permanent marker
- Bench drill
- 3/32-in. drill bit
- Tiger tail jewelry wire, about 60 in.
- Glass beads, assorted
- Crimps and end pieces for jewelry beading
- Fishing tackle parts (a crimp and a snap swivel)
- Pliers

2. Clean the items thoroughly. I used Formula 409 and lots of elbow grease to get the grime off.

3. Decide where you want your chimes to hang from the teapot. For a teapot like this one, I wanted four chimes to hang around the outside perimeter of the teapot and one chime to hang from the center. Mark the holes with a permanent marker.

4. Mark the spots on the top of the teapot where you'd like the beaded strands for hanging. For most teapots, four evenly spaced points will probably be best.

5. Drill each marked hole with the bench drill and drill bit. Also drill a hole at the bottom (stem end) of each piece of silverware.

6. Cut the wire to desired lengths and bead each strand.

7. Attach the silverware to the strands by looping the wire through the holes and attaching with a crimp.

8. Thread the ends of the strands through the holes and affix with crimps or end pieces.

9. In the same way, attach the top beaded strands for hanging.

10. To hold the top strands together for hanging, I used fishing tackle parts. Thread the wire through the crimp, add the snap swivel and then push the wire back through the crimp and close with pliers. Hang and enjoy!

green-roof birdhouse

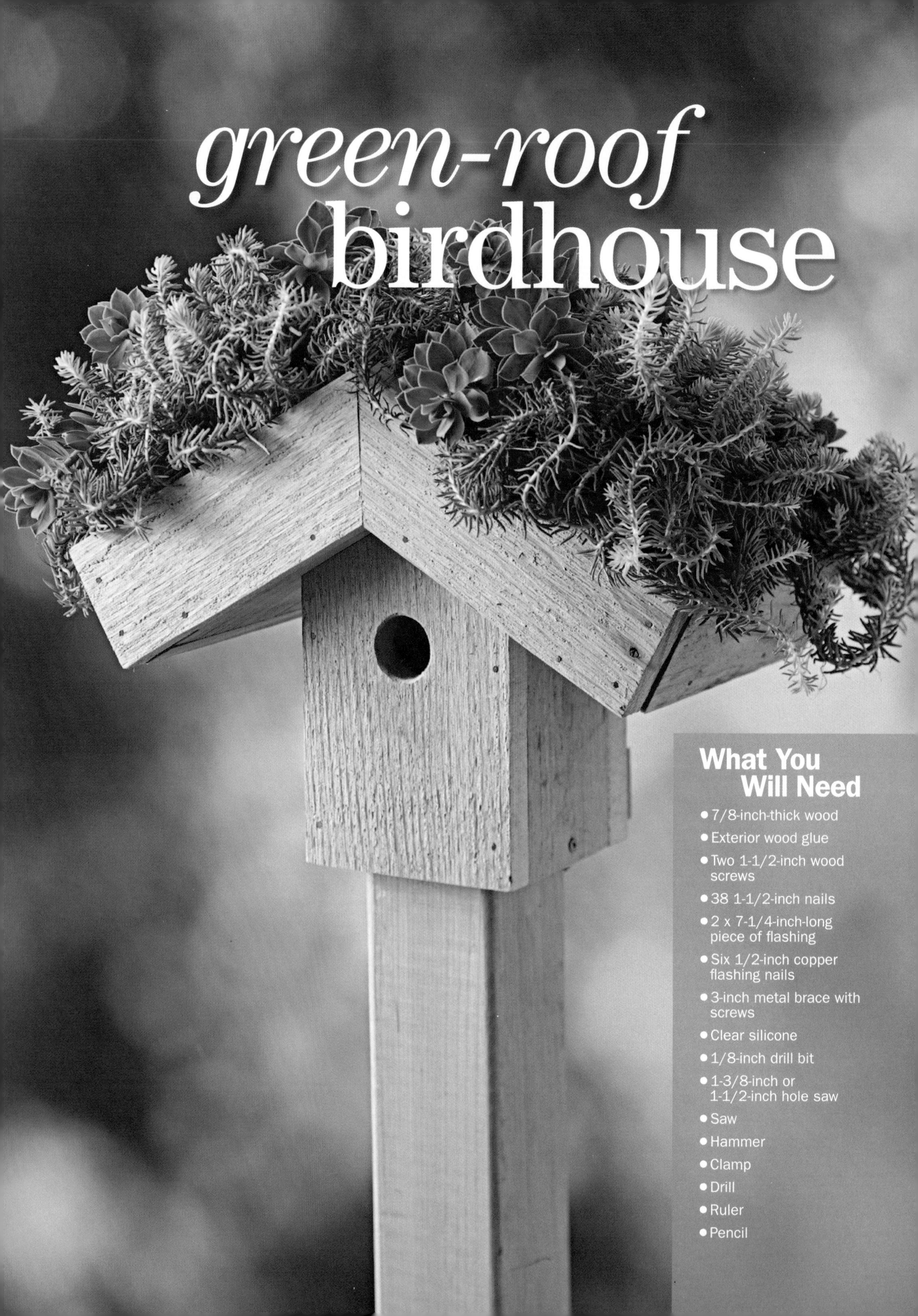

What You Will Need

- 7/8-inch-thick wood
- Exterior wood glue
- Two 1-1/2-inch wood screws
- 38 1-1/2-inch nails
- 2 x 7-1/4-inch-long piece of flashing
- Six 1/2-inch copper flashing nails
- 3-inch metal brace with screws
- Clear silicone
- 1/8-inch drill bit
- 1-3/8-inch or 1-1/2-inch hole saw
- Saw
- Hammer
- Clamp
- Drill
- Ruler
- Pencil

Created by Gary Baltz, article by Dottie Baltz

Bring your birds and plants together with this green-roof birdhouse. It's a clever container idea that also provides a cooler environment for your feathered friends. Best of all, this eco-friendly project takes just a few short hours to complete.

Instructions

1. Cut two pieces of 7/8-inch wood (we used thick rough-sawn cedar) as shown in Diagram A. You will need these for the birdhouse front and back.
2. Cut two side panels measuring 3-3/4 by 6 inches and one bottom measuring 3-1/2 by 3-1/2 inches (Diagram B). Cut about 1/4 inch off each corner of the bottom piece to allow for drainage.
3. Cut two roof panels for your birdhouse, measuring 7-1/4 by 6-1/2 inches (Diagram C).
4. Next, cut the edges of the roof that will hold the soil in place. Cut two right-facing gable pieces and two left-facing pieces as shown in Diagram D. At this time, you'll also need to cut two gable end pieces that measure 3 by 7-1/4 inches, as shown in Diagram E.
5. Finally, make a cleat (this block of wood will go on the lower back of your birdhouse) from scrap lumber by gluing two pieces together so that the result measures about 1-5/8 inches thick by 4 inches long by 1 to 2 inches wide. Use a clamp to hold the pieces together until the glue is dry.
6. Taking one of the panels you cut from Diagram A, measure 5 inches from the bottom center of the panel, and make a small X. Drill through this area using your hole saw to make an entrance hole for the birdhouse.
7. Glue the front and back panels to the side panels from Diagram B so that all pieces

are flush on the bottom. Once the glue has set up, hammer in two siding nails along each side.
8. Take the bottom panel of the birdhouse and tightly fit it up inside. Drill two pilot holes and then attach each side with the wood screws.
9. Run a bead of glue along the peaked edge of the top of the birdhouse base and center the roof panels on top. Secure the roof with two nails along each roofline, for a total of eight nails.

   Once the roof is in place, attach the long metal flashing to the center of the peaked roof using a bead of silicone and six flashing nails. This will prevent water from leaking in on your nesting visitors.
10. Run a bead of wood glue along the edges and attach the gables and the ends to make a box to hold the soil. Use at least two nails on each piece of wood to secure it.
11. To hang the birdhouse, attach a metal mending brace to the back of the top near the peak of the roof. Glue the cleat you made to the bottom of the back of the birdhouse so that the birdhouse will hang flat against a post or tree.

Here are a few extra tips to make your project a success.
- For winter, put your house in the garage, or just replace plants in spring.
- Succulents are a good choice because they do well in shallow soil.
- Moss is a good plant option for birdhouses that will be in shade.
- Put drainage holes in the overhanging area of the roof to avoid root rot in wet weather.

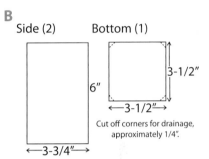

A

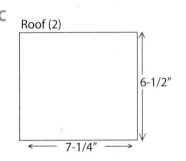

B
Side (2) Bottom (1)

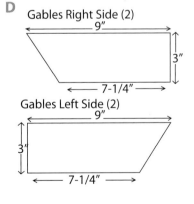

C
Roof (2)

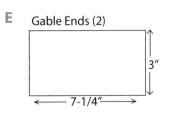

D
Gables Right Side (2)
Gables Left Side (2)

E
Gable Ends (2)

Because all the components are metal or glass, this beauty can adorn your garden year-round, surviving whatever weather brings your way.

upcycled *bird feeder*

Turn old odds and ends into a unique bird feeder. By Beth Evans-Ramos

You don't have to spend a lot of money to have an interesting bird feeder. Just look around your house for a few found objects, then put them together for a whimsical piece of garden art.

Here, crystal chandelier drops add elegance, plumbing parts lend an industrial touch, and the old hubcap that holds the seed is pure genius!

While a feeder like this can take many different shapes, here are a few basics to help you fashion one of your own.

Instructions

1. To begin, look for items to stack that may already have holes or openings in the center.

2. Most likely you will need to punch or drill a hole in the center of your hubcap, just big enough for your threaded rod to slip through. Punch holes through it and any of the other pieces that need a center opening with a heavy-duty metal punch or a hammer and nail.

3. Experiment with stacking your metal pieces. Just start on a flat surface and layer away. It's fun to have a piece to hang things from underneath your hubcap; try a vegetable steamer facing downward for a playful look.

4. When you like your combination, take one of the metal nuts and thread it on the rod about 12 in. below the top. Slide on your bottom piece and add another nut for a secure base.

5. Next, add your hubcap and the other pieces. The best part of this project is that you can change your mind as often as you want!

6. To finish off your stack, slip on the third metal nut and tighten until your pieces stay securely side by side. You might have to adjust the bottom nuts to go higher or lower along the rod.

7. If you don't want the nut on top showing, glue on a finial, such as a hose connector. Use a sturdy, waterproof glue. Two of our favorites are the Marine or Lawn and Garden formula made by Amazing Goop. Both are UV resistant and easy to apply.

8. It's time to embellish with dangles! Suspend camping cups, crystal chandelier drops, beads, bobbins, mystery parts or whatever you fancy from the built-in openings or from holes you punch around the edges of one or more layers. Easy connectors are large paper clips, split rings or binder rings. At first your feathered friends might be timid of the accessories, but give them some time to get used to it.

9. Your threaded rod will slip inside a section of pipe, which can be placed in a garden pot or a bed. If you want a freestanding piece, the rod can slip inside the base and pole of a socket-free, semi-disassembled floor lamp.

10. The only thing left to do is add the bird treats!

What You Will Need

- Threaded rod
- A section of pipe or the bottom portion of a floor lamp (for the base)
- Hubcap, the older the better
- Kitchen steamer
- Lamp parts
- Coffee percolator parts
- Garden hose connections
- Dangles (Step 8)
- Connectors for dangles (Step 8)

footprints
in the sand

Preserve your child's footprints with this mosaic project. By Becky Paton

Instructions

1. Cover the sole of your child's foot with poster paint and have her walk across a sheet of plain paper. When the paint has dried, make a tracing of the best print.

2. Cover a board with brown parcel paper, taping down the sides. Transfer the tracing onto the paper, turning the tracing paper over to make a mirror image for the other foot. Repeat as many times as you like. Cut ceramic tiles into the shape of toes, following a pencil guide drawn onto each, and cut the rest of the tiles into 16ths (use scraps from the toes to make additional 16ths, if needed). Stick the toes down with gum arabic, and outline the foot with the tiny mosaic squares. Have fun with the foot's center, filling it with as many different tiles or objects as you like.

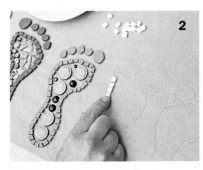

3. After cutting around the footprint with a craft knife, lift the print away and place it onto the casting board, rubbing a small amount of petroleum jelly across its underside to secure it in place.

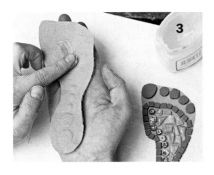

4. Mold Plasticine into a sausage shape, and then roll out a long strip about 3 in. high. Place this around the foot, pressing down the edges to form a secure bond with the board. Gently press the end pieces together so the foot is completely surrounded by a wall of Plasticine. With a brush, paint petroleum jelly around the inside of the Plasticine to act as a release agent.

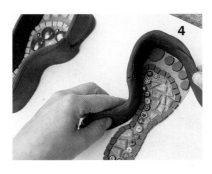

5. In a bowl, mix up the sand and cement with a little PVA and water until you have a thick liquid with the consistency of heavy cream. Remove a little bit of this into another bowl and thin it down further with water. Gently pour the thinner mixture over the foot, pressing it firmly into gaps.

6. Add the rest of the mixture, smoothing the surface. Gently tap the board for a while: The vibrations will release most of the air bubbles in the mixture, ensuring a solid casting.

7. To ensure that the sand and cement set firmly, create an airtight covering around the Plasticine mold with plastic wrap, leaving the foot on a level surface to harden. The plastic wrap will hold in moisture, allowing the sand and cement to dry out very slowly. Let dry for four or five days.

8. Carefully remove the plastic wrap and free the foot from the Plasticine mold by gently easing it away from the sides of the foot. Put the used Plasticine into a sealable bag, as it can be used again.

9. Turn the foot over and gently remove the brown paper on which the tiles were originally placed. This will leave a mirror image of your mosaic design.

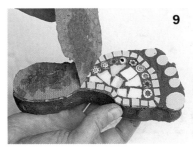

10. The sand and cement are by no means fully set at this stage, but the foot will be strong enough for you to carefully clean any stray mixture off the tops of the tiles using a scouring pad. Place the foot in a resealable bag and allow to dry out very slowly. If it dries too fast, it will crack. Two weeks is a good time to allow.

11. After two weeks, remove the foot from the bag and let it dry out completely in a shady place. If any air holes are visible, grout over the surface and clean in the usual way, bearing in mind that the grout will dry a lot faster than usual as its depth is minimal.

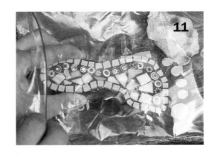

Becky Paton is the author of *Garden Mosaics: 25 Step-by-Step Projects for Your Outdoor Room* (Cico Books, 2010).

This feeder was designed to hold a store-bought suet cake that is still in its plastic tray. If you'd like to try using homemade suet, place it in a plastic tray first to help it keep its shape.

Silverware suet feeder

Treat your birds to an elegant meal served in a feeder made with silver spoons and forks. By Lisa Hilderbrand

Your backyard birds deserve a fine dining experience, so serve up their suet in this elegant yet functional holder for a suet cake. Old silverware holds the suet in place for a whimsical way to feed your birds. It takes only a little while to put together—and before you know it, backyard birds will be lining up for a seat at the table.

What You Will Need

- Weathered board, 2 ft. long and at least 9 in. wide
- Silver-plated flatware, five pieces
- Hinge
- Wire, 18 in. long, 20-gauge
- Screws, assorted sizes to fit hinge holes and drilled silverware
- Drill bits
- Scrap piece of two-by-four
- Drill press or hand drill
- Nail
- Rubber mallet
- Screwdriver
- Wire cutter
- Pliers
- Safety goggles
- Gloves
- Wrapped suet cake

Instructions

1. Pound silverware as flat as you can with a rubber mallet. The more rustic it looks, the better!

2. Use the nail to make divots in handles of the silverware to keep the drill bit from skipping.

3. With safety goggles on, drill holes with drill press or hand drill, keeping drill bit perpendicular to silverware.

4. To make the first bend, place one piece of silverware, decorative side up, on a sturdy surface. Place two-by-four on top of the handle, and bend the silverware up at a 90-degree angle. Wear gloves if you'd like, and repeat with remaining silverware.

5. To determine where silverware should go, place a wrapped suet cake on the weathered board; mark with a pencil. Place silverware on the board to hold suet, and attach with screws.

6. Make the second bend by placing the two-by-four flush with each piece of silverware and bending the silverware over the two-by-four. Refer to photo (right), and use the rubber mallet to help, if necessary.

7. Attach a hinge to the back of the board. The tubular part of the hinge should be just above the edge.

8. String wire through the center of the hinge and curl it with pliers to make decorative loops for hanging.

9. Remove the wrapper from a store-bought suet cake, but leave it in the plastic tray. Insert into the feeder.

10. You're done! Now just enjoy the birds enjoying their treat!

break the mold

Capture the natural beauty of a leaf in this elegant birdbath!

By Dottie Baltz

You don't have to pay a lot for a one-of-a-kind birdbath. This spring, look for plants with large leaves to add to your garden. Then turn one of those big beauties into a birdbath. This project makes a serene resting place for butterflies, too.

Instructions

1. Choose a leaf at least 10 inches long and 7 inches wide. (We used a hosta leaf here, but rhubarb, burdock, gunnera, castor bean, caladium and elephant-ear leaves also work well.) Cut the stem off.

2. Spread out a sheet of plastic or a large plastic bag to protect your work surface. Pour the play sand onto the plastic and make a pile. Wet the sand slightly so that it sticks together, the way you would for a sand castle.

3. Shape the pile to approximate the size and shape of your leaf, but keep in mind that birds do not like baths that are more than a couple of inches deep.

Once the sand pile is to your liking, cover it with a piece of plastic or a plastic bag. Place the leaf vein-side up on top of the plastic, centering it.

4. In a plastic bowl, mix three parts contractor's sand to one part Portland cement. Mix 1/4 cup of water and

What You Will Need

- Large leaf
- 1/2 to 1 bag of play sand
- 3 to 4 cups of contractor's sand
- 1 to 2 cups Portland cement
- Concrete fortifier

Step 3

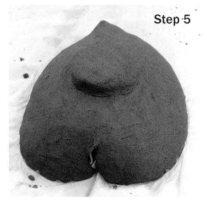
Step 5

Step 7

1/4 cup of concrete fortifier, and add slowly to the sand until it reaches the consistency of a thick brownie batter. The easiest way to do this is to squish it with your hands wearing rubber gloves. Mix more water and fortifier to add to the sand if needed.

Rinse your gloves or hands. Pick up a handful of the sand mixture, plop it on the center of the leaf and spread to the edges. This gives you a solid surface that picks up the leaf's veining while removing air bubbles.

5. Now slowly start building up the thickness of the casting. For strength,

keep it between 1/2 and 1 inch thick. Be careful to keep the edges smooth to get a good contour.

Once you have the casting at a good thickness, build up the center to make a pedestal.

6. Cover the mixture loosely with plastic. If it's a hot day, you might want to mist the casting from time to time to keep it from drying out too fast and cracking.

Let your project dry slowly for about 24 hours, then peel off the leaf. If the casting feels brittle, let it sit for another day.

BIRDBATH MAINTENANCE
You can leave your birdbath out year-round, but if it's painted or stained, you might want to bring it inside during winter. Clean it just as you would any other birdbath, using a sponge or small brush once a week.

7. After the casting has dried for a good week, you can paint or seal it. (We painted this one green.) Or just leave it as is!

JUDYWHITE / GARDENPHOTOS.COM

Growing Veggies

Growing your own vegetables is a healthy and rewarding activity in which the whole family can participate. Try it yourself with these simple, time-saving and frugal tips.

Homegrown on Your Own **224**

60-Minute Veggie Garden **228**

Top 10: Seed-Starting Vegetables **230**

Avoid These 5 Common Mistakes **234**

Contain Yourself **238**

Container Tomatoes **241**

Eat Your Vegetables **242**

Beat the Clock **244**

Homegrown
on your own

Turn your backyard into a mini-farmers market—and save a bushel, too!

By Suzanne DeJohn, National Gardening Association

Just like that sweater in the back of your closet that will one day be fashionable again, kitchen gardens are back in vogue, helping budget-conscious households around the country win the battle against higher prices.

But saving money isn't the only benefit of getting dirt under your fingernails. Few things promote a healthier diet more than growing nutritious, delicious vegetables. Raising your own chemical-free produce can also reduce the carbon footprint left by so-called "food miles," the transportation chain that brings veggies to grocery stores.

You can tailor your garden to fit your tastes: tomatoes, oregano and basil if Italian food's your thing; cilantro, tomatoes, onions, garlic and peppers if Mexican cuisine pleases your palate. Better yet, you'll be amazed at how children or spouses who normally avoid vegetables the way vampires avoid dawn will go gaga over homegrown produce, which is tastier and fresher than store-bought.

Here are some guidelines for getting started.

Creating a Perfect Plot

Whether your yard is big or small, there's always room for veggies. Thoughtful preparation helps minimize the need for chemical intervention down the road. These tips should help you achieve the perfect plot.

Location is key. If you want to convert part of your lawn into a vegetable patch, choose an area in full sun; six hours or more a day is ideal. Morning light is preferable because it

ka-ching! gardens are a good investment

It's hard to tell how much money you save by growing veggies. But Roger Doiron, founder of Kitchen Gardeners International (*kitchengardeners.org*), figures the 834 pounds of produce he grew in a 1,600-square-foot garden in 2008 would've cost $2,196 at a grocery store. Figuring in expenses of $282, that's almost a 700 percent return on investment. He estimates that a more typical-size, 20-by-20 garden could yield $600 worth of produce.

dries dew, which reduces the risk of disease. Also, it puts less stress on plants than blazing afternoon sunlight.

Try a raised bed. Once you choose a location, build a raised bed. The benefits are many: You're assured of high-quality soil with good drainage; tending it is easier on your back; and you can start gardening earlier because the soil warms up faster.

Time to dig in. There's nothing wrong with a ground-level garden, either. Remove existing grass and till the soil; for quick results, use a rototiller. Then remove any grass clumps and blend compost into the top 8 inches of soil. Wait a week or two before planting to allow cultivated soil to settle. Or, if you prefer some aerobic exercise, use a garden spade to lift, turn and prepare the soil to a depth of 8 inches. Amend the spade-prepared soil with compost.

Test first. Healthy soil ensures robust, productive plants. Before planting, test your soil to find out its pH (a measure of acidity/alkalinity) and nutrient level. Regional cooperative extension offices may offer testing services or resources.

Professional tests are better than do-it-yourself kits because you find out what type and amount of fertilizer or amendments you need to add. This includes adjusting pH so the plants are able to absorb the nutrients they need from the soil.

Compost is the best soil amendment; it improves drainage and water-holding capacity. It also adds nutrients and boosts soil life.

Start Plants Off Right

Now comes the fun part—planting time! Keep these simple tips in mind and enjoy healthy, delicious veggies in no time.

Pick your produce. To get the biggest bang for your buck, grow vegetables your family enjoys. Also consider those that are expensive to buy or that are easy to can or store. In addition, choose smaller varieties with "dwarf," "bush" or "compact" in their names so they don't overwhelm their neighbors. There are exceptions, of course; for instance, you can raise sugar snap peas and pole beans on a tepee or trellis.

The easiest vegetables to grow from seed include beans, beets, cucumbers, melons, summer squash and greens, such as chard. Bush-type varieties of beans, cucumbers, melons and squash usually grow faster and take up much less space than vining types. For fast-growing herbs from seed, consider basil, cilantro and dill.

You can also grow favorites such as tomatoes, peppers and eggplant from seeds. But they're slower-growing, "long-season" crops, so most gardeners start seeds indoors six to eight weeks before the average last spring frost date so plants have enough time to mature before the fall frost. Herbs such as sage, rosemary and thyme also require a longer growing season, which makes them good candidates for the starter-plant route.

PLAYING IN THE DIRT. Here's a samping of magic moments along the way as you break ground for your vegetable garden: Turning over soil (top left) and blending in compost to a depth of 8 inches; composting all the grass you removed to create your garden plot, along with any other yard waste (left); giving your garden a good head start by growing seedlings from seeds indoors (top right); and—finally!—transplanting seedlings into your garden (right).

Sowing seeds. You can either sow seeds indoors in late winter or early spring, or plant them directly in the ground when it's warm enough. The latter is the easiest way to plant a veggie garden.

Follow the planting directions on the back of each seed packet. Be prepared to thin plants shortly after they sprout to allow the healthier ones to grow tall and full.

Cover to protect. For a few days after sowing your seeds or setting out your tender seedlings, place lawn chairs over the planting area as a protective canopy against the elements. Other protectors include Reemay and other floating row covers, individual "wall-o'-waters" or milk jugs. Once the plants get their legs under them, remove the protectors. After the soil warms, mulch to retain moisture and help keep weeds at bay, and water regularly.

Then get ready to reap the rewards of your labors. And remember: Saving money and eating better never go out of style.

MAKE IT COUNT WITH A SEASON-LONG HARVEST
Ideally, your kitchen garden should produce over the entire growing season, rather than in one big surge. For a continuous harvest, simply choose plants that meet that goal and follow these tips:

Stagger planting dates. Have extra young plants waiting in the wings, whether you start them from seed a week or so later, or periodically pick up more fresh seedlings to plant as you consume their larger cousins. Do this year-round in mild climates.

Don't let herbs go to seed. Trim them constantly before flowers or flower heads can form.

Use protective barriers. If you garden in deer or woodchuck territory, or host backyard soccer games, erect a protective fence around your garden. Use poultry wire or wood.

If woodchucks tunnel in, just sink the barrier into the ground 18 inches or so. Fencing should stand at least 5 feet for deer and 4 feet for rabbits. If the result is unattractive, plant fast-growing climbing plants to cover it, such as morning glories.

on your mark, get set, grow!

Got an hour to spare?

Then you've got time to create

your first veggie garden. For real.

An estimated 7 million people grabbed pitchforks and shovels in 2009 to put in their first vegetable gardens. They did it to save money. To feel more secure about the safety of their food supply. To enjoy fresher, tastier produce. And maybe, in part, because it's fun to play in the dirt.

Not to put you on the spot, but what's stopping you from joining Locavore Nation this year?

Grace Romero, plant breeder and lead horticulturist for the W. Atlee Burpee & Co. seed business, says you can create a raised-bed veggie garden in 60 minutes. **Seriously.** (*See below right for details.*)

Be Realistic

Novices should keep a few things in mind, Grace notes. While the heavy lifting comes at the beginning and end of the growing season—preparing the soil and planting in spring, then harvesting and putting the garden to bed in fall—there's still much to do in between.

"Begin with the end in mind," Grace says. "When you plan your garden, think about how much time you can dedicate to the plants over the course of the growing season, and how much time you have to get the garden started at the beginning of the season."

How do you know how much time it will take? As a rule of thumb, Grace estimates that it takes 10 hours to excavate, plow and plant a 10-by-10-foot vegetable plot. That same plot will require about two hours each week to maintain and five hours for cleanup after the last harvest. If this sounds too taxing or too daunting, Grace has some hints for cutting down on the time investment.

"For starters, rein in the size of the garden to no larger than 50 or 60 square feet," she suggests. "You can reap a nice harvest from a small garden. Remember that, on average, one modern hybrid beefsteak-type tomato plant yields 40 to 50 tomatoes, and a cherry or grape tomato plant can produce hundreds of fruits."

Give Veggies a Raise

Grace also recommends raised beds, which reduce the need for time-consuming excavation while providing benefits such as improved drainage and easier access for maintenance. Soil in raised beds warms up faster, too, which is a boon for Northern gardeners. You can save even more time by buying easy-to-assemble raised-bed kits.

Here's another time-saving tip: Use vegetable transplants instead of seeds.

"Many gardeners think that in order to grow the latest and greatest new varieties, you have to start from seed," Grace says. "While it's true you won't see the newest introductions available as transplants at your garden center, many newer varieties are available online or in catalogs."

She also suggests installing a drip-irrigation system in your raised bed, which makes watering as effortless as turning on a faucet. Even better, drip irrigation cuts down on waste by ensuring that water goes right where it's needed most: to the thirsty roots.

"Finally, be sure to mulch the bed after everything is planted," Grace says. "Not only will a well-mulched bed keep weeds at bay, it'll also increase moisture retention."

And help keep that precious time on your side.

get your stopwatch ready

Are you primed to take the 60-minute raised-bed challenge? Just follow the step-by-step instructions below, provided by Grace Romero, lead horticulturist for W. Atlee Burpee & Co. Using a ready-to-assemble kit, you'll have a garden in about the same time it takes to watch your favorite TV show. Then kick back and let the good times grow!

STEPS	MINUTES
1. Set out your garden supplies.	7
2. Assemble your 4-by-4-foot raised-bed kit.	15
3. Fill the bed with potting soil, then loosen and spread with a spading fork.	8
4. Plant your transplants, then direct-sow any seeds.	22
5. Thoroughly water the bed and mulch around transplants and over seeds.	8
TOTAL ELAPSED TIME:	**60**

seed-starting veggies

So many choices, so little space. That pretty well sums up a beginning gardener's dilemma, given the vast variety of veggies out there. Bewildered? Here's help. On these pages, you'll find 10 vegetables that provide the best value for your hard-earned dollars. Not only will you save money by growing them from seed instead of buying mature plants, you'll also maximize your yield per square foot of garden. So get ready to sow, hoe and watch your savings grow.

BEETS
Beta vulgaris

The veggie world's unsung heroes, these sweet, nutritious delights are a high-yield crop because they don't take up much space. Their intense color comes from betacyanin, which has cancer-fighting properties, particularly against colon cancer. (For beet-stained hands, try lemon juice.) Whether you eat 'em plain or pickled—or use the green tops for salads—you can't beat beets for a healthy treat.

Hardiness: Grown as an annual.

Light needs: Full sun.

Ready to harvest: 49 to 56 days.

Fruit color: Deep red, maroon, purple, gold and white.

Planting advice: Beet seeds are clustered in a dried fruit that produces several seedlings. Plant about ½ inch deep and 1 inch apart, with 12 to 18 inches between rows. Thin out seedlings so they're 1 to 3 inches apart. For an extended harvest, plant a crop every three to four weeks through midsummer. Pull mature fruits when they're 1½ to 3 inches in diameter.

Recommendations: Little Ball (miniature), Green Top Bunching and Crosby Egyptian (for tasty greens).

BROCCOLI

Brassica oleracea

A member of the cabbage family, broccoli thrives in cooler weather. With that in mind, grow your own seedlings and transplant them in early spring so they have time to mature. Or plant in summer for a fall harvest when temps drop. Then get ready for good eating with this crowd pleaser, which is rich in vitamins A and D.

Hardiness: Grown as an annual.

Light needs: Full sun.

Ready to harvest: 55 to 65 days.

Fruit color: Green.

Planting advice: Plant seeds ¼ to ½ inch deep and about 18 inches apart; plant seedlings a little deeper than they were set indoors. Space rows 36 inches apart. A central green head develops first; harvest it when it's about 4 to 6 inches in diameter. This will also give it time to produce tender, tasty side shoots.

Recommendations: Cruiser (heat-tolerant), Green Goliath, Green Comet.

CARROTS

Daucus carota

Biting into a crisp, freshly pulled carrot is one of gardening's sublime pleasures. They're rich in carotene—a source of valuable vitamin A—and a good source of fiber. Better yet, kids love that satisfying crunch.

Hardiness: Grown as an annual.

Light needs: Full sun.

Ready to harvest: 50 to 75 days, depending on variety.

Fruit color: Orange, white, yellow, red, purple.

Planting advice: Plant seeds ¼ to ½ inch deep, with two to three seeds per inch. Keep rows about 12 to 18 inches apart. When the seedlings are an inch tall, thin them so you have only two per inch for smaller varieties and one to two per inch for larger varieties. You'll want to thin again as the carrot plants grow taller.

Recommendations (from small to large): Thumbelina (good for container gardening), Royal Chantenay, Scarlet Nantes, Legend.

CUCUMBERS

Cucumis sativus

With their sprawling vines, when do cucumbers become champion producers by the square foot? When you grow them vertically on a trellis, of course. These juicy veggies are mostly water inside; the mineral-rich skin packs more nutritional value. But talk about versatility: The fruit also contains skin-soothing vitamin C and caffeic acid, which is why the gals at the spa insist on putting slices of them over your eyes during a facial.

Hardiness: Grown as an annual.

Light needs: Full sun.

Ready to harvest: 55 to 68 days.

Fruit color: Green.

Planting advice: Sow seeds ½ to 1 inch deep and thin seedlings to one every 12 inches; or plant transplants 1 to 2 feet apart, in rows spaced 5 or 6 feet apart. For slicing, pick when they're about 2 inches in diameter and up to 10 inches long, and before they turn yellow.

Recommendations: Bush Crop and Fanfare (compact varieties), Burpless (trellis-friendly), Straight 8.

HEIRLOOM TOMATOES

Lycopersicon lycopersicum

In a popularity poll, these red wonders win in a landslide. In fact, it's estimated that one-third of all garden plants sold in the United States are tomatoes. Whether you prefer them cut in chunks and sprinkled with salt, sliced and piled high on a sandwich, diced and tossed in chili or stew or pureed for homemade sauce, nothing else tastes like a garden tomato. And if you grow these delectable old-fashioned varieties from seed, the varieties are almost limitless.

Hardiness: Grown as an annual.

Light needs: Full sun.

Ready to harvest: Varies by variety.

Fruit color: Red, green, white, yellow, pink, purple, orange, striped.

Planting advice: Seeds can be sown in flats or in individual containers. They transplant easily; just set tall, leggy transplants a bit deeper in the garden for better rooting, about 2 to 3 feet apart.

Recommendations: Cherokee Purple, Brandywine (an old Amish variety).

ONIONS

Allium cepa

Easy to grow and good for your heart, onions add sass to any recipe. What's better on a burger than a thick slice of freshly harvested onion (with a side of breath freshener, of course)? As a plus, their powerful odor deters many garden pests.

Hardiness: Grown as an annual.

Light needs: Full sun.

Ready to harvest: 100 to 120 days.

Fruit color: White, red, yellow.

Planting advice: While growing from seed allows more choices, gardeners typically find it easier planting onions as sets, which are small bulbs less than 1 inch in diameter. Onions thrive in cooler weather, so plant the sets in early spring, about 1 inch deep and 2 to 4 inches apart. Space rows about 18 inches apart. When the tops dry and fall over, it's time to pull them out and cure them for winter storage.

Recommendations: Select varieties suited to your region (there are northern and southern onions). Try Sweet Spanish, Bermuda, Vidalia, Walla Walla, Red Baron.

PEPPERS

Capsicum annuum

From sweet, crisp bell peppers to fiery habaneros, festive peppers are the life of the garden party. They add color and flavor to salads, soups, stews, salsas and more. Muy bueno!

Hardiness: Grown as an annual.

Light needs: Full sun.

Ready to harvest: 70 to 75 days.

Fruit color: Green, red, yellow, orange, brown, purple, black.

Planting advice: Set transplants about 18 to 24 inches apart in fertile, well-draining soil. Consistent, uniform watering is a must throughout the growing season.

Recommendations: Purple Belle, Sweet Banana, Cayenne, Jalapeno, Bell Boy.

SNAP BEANS

Phaseolus vulgaris

Easy to grow and available in bush and climbing varieties, snap beans are on most gardeners' A-lists. And talk about productive: A 100-foot-long row of healthy plants can yield 75 pounds of beans. For even better yields, grow pole beans that produce an extra picking and can be trained to grow on a trellis or fence, which leaves room for other produce.

Hardiness: Grown as an annual.

Light needs: Full sun.

Ready to harvest: 45 to 65 days.

Fruit color: Green, yellow, purple.

Planting advice: Plant bush bean seeds 1 inch deep and 2 to 4 inches apart. Rows should be 18 to 24 inches apart. Plant pole bean seeds 4 to 6 inches apart, with rows 36 inches apart. Pick them before the seeds inside the pod grow too big, lest they get tough and stringy.

Recommendations: Blue Lake, Kentucky Wonder.

SUGAR SNAP PEAS

Lathyrus odoratus

Peas don't get much respect, but they should: They're packed with vitamins and other nutrients, such as folic acid, which is good for bone and cardio-vascular health. Kids may turn up their noses at the funny, round little pellets—but they just might love snacking on the crisp, freshly picked pods instead.

Hardiness: Grown as an annual.

Light needs: Full sun.

Ready to harvest: 65 to 75 days.

Fruit color: Green.

Planting advice: Peas don't mind cooler weather, so there's no harm in planting them earlier than other veggies. Sow seeds about 1 inch deep and 1 inch apart. Allow 18 to 24 inches between rows. Harvest before the seeds inside the pod get too big.

Recommendations: Sugar Daddy, Sugar Ann, Super Sugar Snap.

SUMMER SQUASH

Cucurbita pepo

Anyone who's ever received zucchini from an overwhelmed neighbor knows these veggies are prolific growers. Unlike fall and winter squash, they don't need much space to produce an abundant harvest. They come in many shapes, colors and varieties, including zucchini, yellow crookneck and scallop. And for dinner, don't forget the flowers, which are edible, too.

Hardiness: Grown as an annual.

Light needs: Full sun.

Ready to harvest: 50 to 60 days.

Fruit color: Black, green, yellow.

Planting advice: In well-draining soil, sow several seeds about 2 inches apart, or four or five in a 1-inch-tall hill. Thin them to one robust plant or roughly two per hill when they're 2 or 3 inches tall. Harvest the long, narrow varieties when they're no more than 2 inches in diameter and 6 to 8 inches long, or they'll be tough as leather. And wear gloves; the stalks are prickly.

Recommendations: Sundance (crookneck), Aristocrat (zucchini), Goldbar (straightneck), Peter Pan (scallop variety).

Avoid 5 these Common Mistakes

Time is money—and you can save both by following these simple suggestions.

You're bound to err when you take your first stab at vegetable gardening. But don't worry. As a smart guy by the name of Albert Einstein once said, "Anyone who has never made a mistake has never tried anything new."

Not that we advocate making preventable errors. After all, gardening blunders cost you both time and money. So with that in mind, we asked Bill Rein, a horticulturist at the venerable W. Atlee Burpee & Co., to point out five common missteps that beginning gardeners make. After that, feel free to make your own mistakes and learn from them.

1 Great expectations

High on their own enthusiasm, many veggie gardeners bite off more than they can chew by planting gardens without considering the time and effort needed to maintain them.

"You have to remember that plants are living things, so neglect—unless you're very lucky—means dead plants or, at the very least, sad-looking plants," Bill says. "Be realistic about how much time you have for gardening, and refrain from growing more than you can maintain. A small, healthy garden is a lot more attractive than loads of wilting plants among a mass of weeds."

And too much maintenance can be as bad as too little. "Some of the new gardeners I've met during my travels are so dedicated that they actually end up overdoing it: overwatering, overfertilizing and overpruning," Bill notes. "It's easy to do if you really enjoy tinkering in the garden."

To avoid showering your plants with too much attention, draw up a weekly checklist of maintenance tasks and stick to it.

2 Ignoring light requirements

It sounds simple enough: Locate plants that need full sun in sunny areas and those that prefer shade in shady areas.

"But you'd be surprised at how many gardeners, new and old, get this wrong," Bill says.

Full sun actually means the plant grows best in six or more hours of direct sunlight. Sure, you can plant it in a spot that gets less than six hours, but the chances are your yield will decrease and the fruits won't be nearly as sweet, Bill warns.

To avoid making this mistake with the area you're considering, track the sunlight in that spot for about a week before you plant. This should give you enough time to observe the way light hits your yard on both sunny and cloudy days. If you monitor sunlight in early spring, be sure to account for how much shade nearby trees will produce after they fully leaf out.

If you don't have time or aren't at home enough to make such observations, try a digital monitor like the SunCalc.

3 Forgetting to make amends

"Amending the soil is the first and most important task before you start planting," Bill says. "I can't stress enough how important it is to prepare the planting site."

Good soil means the right combination of silt, clay, and organic material. Too much sand in the soil can dry your plants out. Compact soils with too much clay can lead to poor air and water circulation.

Start by digging the bed, then removing weeds, debris and rocks so you can see and touch the soil. Grab a handful. Does it feel compacted or gummy, or does it appear to be exceptionally loose and grainy, indicating a sandy soil type?

"For sandy soil, add a higher ratio of organic material," Bill recommends. "Place at least 2 inches on top of the bed and work it in evenly to a depth of 4 to 6 inches. For clay soil, you should work in an ample amount of compost, so that the clay-to-organic-material ratio is roughly 50-50."

Adding organic matter improves your soil's texture and nutrient balance. But you also can get a soil test by taking samples to your local university extension office. Soil tests are helpful because they indicate which nutrients your soil lacks and what should be added, as well as the soil's pH level and what should be done to change it. Then you can remedy the situation accordingly.

4 Assuming more fertilizer is better

"There are lots of new and longtime gardeners who burn up their lawns and plants by being heavy-handed with fertilizer," Bill says. "It's an easy mistake to make, but it's also easy to avoid if you just take the time to understand how fertilizer works."

Plants, like people, require balanced nutrition. Just as humans can overdose on vitamins or other supplements, plants can get sick or even die by taking in too much of one or more nutrients.

"A gardener reads the fertilizer rate on the back of the bottle or bag and decides that adding a bit more than recommended will speed up the results," Bill observes. "A few days later, dramatic results aren't visible, so the gardener decides to add just a bit more fertilizer. Before you know it, the plants begin to show results—they start to turn brown."

Plants can metabolize only so much before they literally overdose. To avoid overfeeding, Bill recommends following fertilizer instructions to the letter. That means adding only the recommended amount as often as the label instructs.

"Remember that some fertilizers are designed to feed gradually," Bill points out. "There's no need to reapply if the fertilizer is continuously releasing nutrients into the soil. Just because you can't see it doesn't mean it's not working."

5 Willy-nilly watering

"Most first-year gardeners fall into two categories: overattentive or neglectful," Bill says. "The overattentive bunch waters way too frequently and often ends up with root rot. The neglectful group forgets to keep up with regular watering and ends up with dried-up, wilting plants."

Bill recommends that gardeners test soil moisture by simply placing a finger about an inch or so into the soil. If it feels dry, go ahead and water thoroughly. If it feels moist, wait a day and check again.

Here's another thing to avoid: watering above the plants.

"Sure, it's easier to water above the plants, but it's not very efficient," Bill says. "In fact, it can cause leaf spot and blight problems."

It's best to place a hose nozzle atop the soil, directly over a plant's roots, and allow just a trickle of water to be absorbed into the soil. Or set your hose nozzle to the "soaker" setting, then manually water the base of the plant.

"If you're really concerned about minimizing water waste while still watering effectively, install a drip-irrigation system in your garden," Bill suggests. "It's a worthwhile investment for plants that require consistent watering, such as vegetables."

Consistency is another key. "Consistent watering is critical to disease resistance and the development of root systems," Bill says.

Livestock farms are a good source of free manure. Just be sure it's not fresh: The high ammonia content can harm veggies—and neighbors might raise a stink about the odor!

Water deeply and less often instead of more frequent, shallow watering. Thorough watering encourages plants to grow deep, water-seeking roots that can gather moisture from a larger area.

contain yourself

Containers provide urban veggie gardeners with room to grow. By William Moss, National Gardening Association

It's easy to see how city dwellers might feel left out of the veggie-gardening party. But even gardeners with small spaces can raise enough nutritious produce to prepare a few meals and enhance their diets—not to mention trim their grocery bills. In fact, with a little planning and attention, container gardens can produce like mini-farms.

Getting started doesn't require a home-equity line of credit, either. Almost any vessel can be used as a container, as long as it has drainage holes that allow water to flow freely through the pot.

Most veggies need only about 6 inches of soil depth. Trays and smaller containers work fine for lettuce, radishes, spinach and peppers.

But root crops, such as carrots and onions, as well as large plants like most tomatoes and squash, require half-barrels, grow bags or other containers larger than 16 inches in diameter. As a general rule, bigger is better for strong root growth and overall vigor.

Packaged potting mixes typically work best. In congested areas where there's a potential for contamination, it's out of the question to fill a container for edibles with city dirt. Commercial mixes are lightweight, moisture-retentive, properly aerated and free of the fungi, bacteria, insects and weed seeds that can cause problems later.

Here Comes the Sun

Sunlight, not space, is probably the biggest challenge for the urban gardener. Without at least six hours of sunlight a day, it's tough to grow quality produce. Crops need a lot of sunshine to produce nutritious fruits, seeds and leaves. Southern exposure is best, but six hours from any direction is sufficient.

Wind exposure is another factor to consider. To prevent soil from drying out and plants from sustaining damage, place large plants in sheltered locations. Avoid narrow alleys or other spots where wind is funneled directly toward the plants. If the only options are exposed balconies and terraces, use wire cages or other sturdy supports to protect big plants like tomatoes, beans, peas and squash.

Give 'Em Some Attention

Regular watering is crucial with containers, because there's limited soil mass for storing water. During the peak of summer heat, you may need to water daily to keep plants growing at full potential. A drip-irrigation system allows you to water automatically; with a timer, you can water containers even while you're away. However, reliable neighbors are always the best option for vacation watering. And if they happen to be master gardeners, then all the better!

Container veggies also need regular fertilizing. Follow the label instructions and make sure the container drains well, or plants may suffer from high salt concentrations as fertilizer builds up. Some gardeners combine the two tasks and simply water with a quarter-strength fertilizer solution once a week.

Chive

For a container garden that combines both good looks and great taste, mix veggies and flowers to create a mini ornamental edible garden.

If plants don't look vigorous and healthy, check them closely, because diseases and pest infestations can quickly get out of hand. If caught early, most are easy to treat. Check the undersides of leaves for insects, many of which can simply be picked off or sprayed away with a strong stream of water.

Some pests require other treatments. Natural insecticides and biological controls (ladybugs, parasitic wasps, predatory midges, etc.) are very popular with eco-minded home gardeners. Always read any product labels to make sure the treatment is compatible with food crops, and follow the directions carefully.

Select Healthy Seedlings

When you select plants, look for vigorous young seedlings with bushy growth. Plants that are lanky or already flowering are not good choices. Check to make sure each seedling is securely anchored in the six-pack or pot, which suggests a well-established root system.

To plant, dip each seedling in a bucket of water to moisten its root ball, tease out any circling roots, and plant it at the same depth it was previously growing. Tomatoes are an exception: You can plant them with the bare stem several inches below the ground, and roots will form along the stem.

Some crops, like lettuce, beets and carrots, are best grown from seed. Simply follow the instructions on the packet. Be sure to thin sprouts to the recommended spacing. Thinning may feel ruthless to you, but fortunately most veggie sprouts can be used in salads and other dishes for an early-season treat.

By following these simple guidelines, you'll see how easy and rewarding it is to grow your own veggies in small spaces.

To avoid container-garden veggies that lean or grow unevenly, give this idea a spin: Rotate the containers weekly for even sun exposure.

Top picks for small spaces

The varieties listed below are good choices for containers. As container gardening grows in popularity, many more options appear every year. To stay up to speed, check garden centers, farmers markets and botanical gardens to see what's new.

Beans: Bush Romano, Bush Blue Lake, Royal Burgundy, Blue Lake.

Carrots: Danvers Half Long, Tiny Sweet, Little Finger, Thumbelina.

Chard: most varieties.

Cucumbers: Patio Pik, Salad Bush Hybrid, Early Pik.

Eggplant: Slim Jim, Ichiban, Black Beauty, Morden Midget.

Lettuce: leaf varieties.

Onions: Japanese Bunching, Beltsville Bunching.

Peppers: Sweet Banana, Cayenne, Yolo Wonder, Jalapeno, Thai Hot, Keystone Resistant.

Spinach: most varieties.

Squash: Scallopini, Early Yellow Summer, Gold Rush.

Tomatoes: Patio VF, Sungold, Early Girl, Sweet 100 Patio, Saladette, Tiny Tim, Pixie II and most determinant varieties.

container tomatoes

By National Gardening Association Editors

It may seem unlikely, but tomatoes can endure mighty close quarters and still deliver the goods. Even if you have room for nothing more than a hanging planter or a bushel basket to place in a sunny spot, indoors or out, you can grow tomatoes like a pro.

Here are some pointers to get you on your way to tasty homemade tomato sauce.

Sun. Container tomatoes need at least six to eight hours of sunshine a day to produce a worthwhile harvest. If you grow them indoors, put them where they'll get maximum sunshine. If necessary, move the container from window to window.

Soil. For hanging planters and small pots, use regular potting soil. With larger containers, you may want to use a lighter-weight, soilless growing mix, such as Jiffy-Mix or Pro-Mix. These retain moisture well, which is important for tomatoes. Garden soil is OK but needs to be lightened with peat moss, vermiculite or perlite to improve its drainage.

Containers. Almost anything will do. You can have a great crop from a plant in a 5-gallon bucket or pot, a smaller hanging planter or even a bushel basket. Just be sure the container has drainage holes in the bottom.

Line bushel baskets with plastic bags (don't forget to poke a few drainage holes) or old nylon stockings to keep the dirt in and retain moisture. Three tomato plants in a bushel basket, supported by short stakes, look pretty on a deck.

Top Varieties. Dwarf varieties are best for containers. If you're trying container growing for the first time, try a cherry patio type, such as Tiny Tim or Pixie II. They need little support—you even can let them trail from a hanging container—and they'll produce fruit early.

Planting. Choose sturdy, stocky transplants and set them in soil up to the bottom set of leaves.

Water. Container tomatoes need more frequent watering because the roots can't reach for extra moisture as garden tomatoes do. In the heat of summer, water daily.

Fertilizer. Mix a small amount of soluble, balanced fertilizer into the plants' water every week or so. Tomatoes like regular feedings of small amounts of fertilizer rather than infrequent large doses.

Pollination. When the plants have flowered, give them a little shake in the middle of the day to aid pollination.

eat *your* vegetables!

Feed your body homegrown goodies and discover a healthier you.

While it's not exactly breaking news that veggies are good for you, many of us still aren't getting enough of them.

Why not? "My kids (or spouse) won't eat them." "I don't have the time or know-how to cook fresh veggies." "Fresh produce is expensive."

But consider this: Calorie for calorie, vegetables pack the biggest nutritional punch of any food you consume daily.

According to current dietary guidelines suggested by the Department of Health and Human Services and the Department of Agriculture, the average person should be eating 2½ cups of vegetables a day. More specifically, we should select from all five vegetable subgroups (dark green, orange, legumes, starchy vegetables and other vegetables) several times a week.

The weekly recommendations are as follows:

Dark green vegetables .... 3 cups
Orange vegetables .... 2 cups
Legumes (dry beans) .... 3 cups
Starchy vegetables.. 3 cups
Other vegetables ....6½ cups

The takeaway? Vary your veggies. Instead of iceberg lettuce, try darker greens such as spinach or collards.

Replace ordinary baked potatoes with sweet potatoes or roasted butternut squash. Choose spaghetti squash in lieu of spaghetti.

And you may find that it's fun to shake up the way you prepare your harvest. Healthy preparation methods include steaming, lightly grilling or eating veggies raw. But roasting and sautéing are also fine, as long as you don't overdo the butter or oil.

So how, specifically, do vegetables benefit the body? Here's an overview:

A better bean

The Scarecrow in *The Wizard of Oz* knew it well: The brain is the body's control panel, so you have to keep it in optimal condition. A diet rich in vegetable antioxidants, like vitamins A, C and E, can help protect your brain from damaging free radicals and decrease age-related memory loss.

Perfect peepers

Everyone knows the vitamin A in carrots promotes good eyesight. But how? By improving night vision and our ability to adjust from bright lights to dim, for a start. But there's more.

Vitamin C helps prevent cataracts. Carotenoids found in dark leafy greens and orange veggies may decrease the risk of developing age-related retinal degeneration.

Vitamin A superfoods include carrots, squash, sweet potatoes, broccoli, pumpkin, spinach and melons. Tomatoes, potatoes, cauliflower and green vegetables are great sources of vitamin C.

Bright smile, strong bones.

The hype is true—you can't have strong bones without calcium. And the same goes for those pearly whites! Until the age of 30-35, your body uses calcium to grow bones and make them as dense as possible. After that, if you're not getting enough calcium, your body steals it from your bones to perform other necessary functions.

Sure, dairy products are the obvious choice for calcium, but you can also beef up your bones with calcium-rich choices like spinach, kale, broccoli and green beans.

Did you know? According to the American Dental Association, vegetables like celery, carrots, cauliflower and cucumbers all also help produce saliva, which combines with the veggies' natural fibers to help clean teeth and remove bacteria.

Glowing skin

Your body's largest organ is your skin. Eating a balanced diet and drinking plenty of water are key to overall health and a glowing complexion. Especially important? Antioxidant vitamins A, C and E, which combat free radicals' aging effects, repair and heal skin, boost collagen production, and protect against sun damage.

Turn to carrots, squash, sweet potatoes, broccoli, pumpkin, spinach and melons for vitamin A, and tomatoes, potatoes, cauliflower and green vegetables for vitamin C. Vitamin E superfoods include seeds—like sunflower and pumpkin—as well as asparagus and cabbage.

ORGANIC—WHEN IT MATTERS MOST

According to the research done by the Environmental Working Group, some fruits and veggies carry more chemicals and pesticides than others, so it's best to grow your own:

peaches	apples
sweet bell peppers	celery
nectarines	strawberries
cherries	lettuce
grapes	spinach
potatoes	pears

beat the clock

Give Mother Nature the cold shoulder and extend your gardening season with these tips. By Natalie Newman

When you're serious about your green thumb, the vegetable gardening season is a lot like watching a season of your favorite TV show: It's over all too soon—and you can't wait until next year.

It doesn't have to be that way. Even novice gardeners can slip one past Mother Nature and extend the "shoulder seasons" of late spring and early fall. And it's not brain surgery, either. Just follow these easy, practical tips, and put time on your side for a change.

Don't forget about
fast-maturing vegetable
varieties. In short summers,
they guarantee a harvest
before the first frost; in
warmer climates with longer
growing seasons, they make
it easier to plant two
rounds of produce.

ENJOY AN ENDLESS SUMMER
(Clockwise from upper left): To protect individual plants, try cloches of plastic or glass. Heirloom varieties may be a smart choice since some mature more slowly—look for varieties that ripen over a long period of time. Use cold frames to extend the season, overwinter some crops and get a jump on next season. For a continuous harvest, stagger the start dates of your spring plantings.

Cold Comfort

It's disappointing when cold weather unexpectedly moves in and damages your plants, but there are ways to cheat the season.

Covers capture and retain the sun's heat around the plant while maintaining soil temperature, which helps nurture growing, ripening vegetables. The solution can be as simple as covering plants with a blanket on a frosty night, or as complex as building a cold frame.

To help individual plants, try cloches of plastic or glass; just remove them at midday if the plants appear to be overheating, and be sure they're on overnight. A nifty plastic cone contraption called a "Wall-o-Water" is also a good option. Available at garden centers or from mail-order suppliers, it lets you use water for insulation.

Another favorite is a cold frame. You can buy a ready-made one, save money with a kit or even build one yourself from wood and an old glass window. It will protect plants at night and in cold weather. Whether you buy or build, make sure the lid can open and close.

You can use these protective techniques in early spring, too, if you want to give your crops a head start.

A Staggering Success

For a continuous harvest, simply stagger the start dates of your spring plantings instead of putting in everything at once. For example, plant half your vegetables around Memorial Day, and a second round a week or even two weeks later. Or plant a row every week for four or five weeks.

Once you've enjoyed the fruits of successive sowing, you can get more sophisticated. At the very least, label rows in the garden with start dates, so you remember what you planted and when. If your garden is large and you feel ambitious, track everything on a computer spreadsheet.

Smart Choices

Have you ever wondered why all your tomatoes or green beans ripen at once? Most likely it's because you grow only one variety. Here are two easy ways around this problem:

Grow several varieties. When you read seed catalogs or stand at the seed rack in the garden store, read the fine print, in particular the "days to maturity." This is an estimate of how long it takes from sowing to harvest, though results may vary somewhat depending on region and weather.

Pick two or more varieties with significantly different maturity periods. Or stagger the planting types—pole beans versus bush beans, for instance. That way, you can plant everything at the same time but enjoy an extended harvest.

Try heirloom varieties. Many modern vegetables are bred to ripen all at once, or over just a few days. Old-fashioned cultivars, however, are quirkier and may germinate or mature more slowly. For example, Brandywine tomatoes may ripen over several weeks. All you have to do is check periodically and pick only the ripe ones.

Keep Track

Even small veggie patches benefit if you keep a gardening journal. Take notes all season on the varieties you grow (including the suppliers' days-to-maturity figures mentioned above), the dates you plant and harvest, susceptibility to pests or diseases, weather conditions and any other details you learn along the way.

This information will serve you well in future seasons as you make smarter decisions about selection and care in your own garden. Tailoring your efforts to your growing conditions means the biggest and best harvests.

get cracking on your own cold frame

If you don't have a greenhouse, a cold frame is the next thing. Essentially, a cold frame is a mini greenhouse that protects plants from chilling winds and low temperatures. Here's some advice on building your own from Charlie Nardozzi of the National Gardening Association.

KEEP IT SIMPLE

The simplest cold frame consists of six hay bales arranged in a rectangle on the southern side of the house and topped with a storm window. Plant in the space in the center of the bales underneath the glass.

REUSE, RECYCLE

If you have an old storm window and some planks or scrap lumber, you can put together another easy cold frame. Nail the wood together to fit as the base under the storm window. Skip the hinges—on hot days, slide the window to the side or prop it up with something to let heat out. On cold nights, cover the window with an old blanket.

WHAT TO PLANT

It's best to plant cool season crops in early fall in your cold frame. Unless you're in the South, there won't be much growth in late fall and winter. However, some crops, such as spinach and kale, can overwinter in a cold frame in a cold climate and be one of the first crops you harvest in spring.

Index

A

Admiral, 192
  red, 196
  white, 193
Agastache, 52
Alaska Botanical Garden, 171
Albany Pine Bush Preserve, 161
Allen, Tom
  host plants for butterflies, 192-193
  perennials for butterflies, 194
  spring butterflies, 196
Amaranth, 53
Annuals, 64-67, 124
  for birds, 56
  for shade, 143
Apples, 197, 243
Art, garden, 44-49, 61, 149, 202-207, 210-211
Ash, mountain, 19
Asparagus, 243
Aster, 124, 180, 193-194
  New England, 180
Astilbe, 142
Atlanta Botanical Garden, 157
Azalea, 137

B

Bachelor's buttons, 56, 122
Barberry, 19
Beans, 139, 240
  snap, 233
Bee
  bumble, 190
  honeybee, 190
  virescent green metallic, 190
Bee balm, 99, 104, 183
Beetle
  milkweed leaf, 190
  Pennsylvania leatherwing, 190
  red milkweed, 190
Beets, 230
Begonia, 143
Bellevue Botanical Garden, 157, 170
Berries, for birds, 19
Betty Ford Alpine Gardens, 156
Bird feeders, 18, 55, 57, 59, 149, 209, 214-215, 218-219
  cleaning, 114
  hummingbird, 94-95

  oriole, 209
  recycled, 214-215
  suet, 218-219
Bird feeding, 18-19, 38-39, 55, 57
  by hand, 95
  oriole, 209
Birdbaths, 18, 39, 48, 61, 220-221
Birdhouse, 149, 212-213
Birding Drives Dakota, 175
Birding trails, 172-175
Birding, urban, 21-23
Birds
  attracting, 16-19, 21-23, 53, 56, 96-101, 120-125, 214-215, 218-219
  food for, 18-19, 55, 57, 130-133
  nesting, 12-15
  photography, 70-73, 80-83
  shelter for, 18, 130-133
  watching and cats, 39
Birdseed, 57
Birmingham Botanical Gardens, 170
Black-eyed Susan, 53, 56
Blackberry, 197
Blanketflower, 67
Blazing star, meadow, 181
Blueberry, northland highbush, 197
Bluebird, 19, 26, 39
  attracting, 39
  eastern, 32-33
  food for, 39
  nesting, 39
Bobwhite, northern, 19
Botanic gardens, 154-157, 170-171
Bowman's Hill Wildflower Preserve, 161
Broccoli, 139, 231, 243
Brooklyn Botanic Garden, 170
Browallia, 143
Brunnera, 142
Budget
  birding, 55, 56-62, 209, 214-215, 218-219
  gardening, 44-49, 50-53, 55-62, 64-67, 149, 202-207, 210-211, 225-227
  travel, 168-171
Bulbs, 137, 147
Bunting
  indigo, 19
  painted, 33
Bush, butterfly, 67, 183, 194-195

Butterfly, 132, 188, 196
  attracting, 120-125, 129, 143, 180-183, 192-193, 194-195, 197
  hairstreak, 123
  Henry's elfin, 122
  host plants, 122-123, 192-195
  painted lady, 122-123
  skipper, 123
  spring azure, 122-123
  swallowtail, 123
Butterfly bush, 67, 183, 194-195

C

Cabbage, 243
Caliente coreopsis, 105
California Central Coast Birding Trail, 175
Canna, 67
Cardinal, northern, 16, 19, 28
Cardinal flower, 99, 105
Carrots, 139, 231, 239-240, 243
Catbird, gray, 19
Catmint, 67
Cats, bird-watching for, 39
Celery, 243
Celosia, 67
Chard, 240
Checkerspot, 193
Cherry, 243
Cheyenne Botanic Gardens, 171
Chicago Botanic Garden, 171
Chickadee, 19
  black-capped, 26
Chokeberry, 19, 197
Chrysanthemum, 124
Cigar plant, 99
Clematis, 124
Cleome, 56, 67, 122-123
Clover, 193
Coleus, 143
Columbine, 104
Composting, 63, 226
Coneflower, 105, 124, 128, 194
  purple, 53, 195
Containers, 46, 61, 62, 106-107, 147, 182-183, 204, 207, 239-241
  for attracting butterflies, 182-183
  for attracting hummingbirds, 106-107

Coot, American, 14
Coral bells, 105, 143
Coreopsis, 53, 105
Cosmos, 56, 66, 124, 128
Cowbird, brown-headed, 14–15
Crabapple, 19, 129
Cranberry, highbush, 19
Crapemyrtle, 136
Crescents, 193
Cricket, snowy tree, 191
Croton, 67
Cucumber, 231, 240

D

Dahlias, 165
Daisies, Dahlberg, 56, 67
Daylily, 104, 129
Delphinium, 165
Denver Botanic Garden, 154–157
Dewberry, 197
Dogwood, 122
    Cornelian cherry, 137
    pagoda, 19
Dove, 19
Dowagiac Woods Nature Sanctuary, 161
Dragonfly
    green darner, 189
    twelve-spotted skimmer, 189
    widow skimmer, 189

E

Eagle, bald, 12–13, 29
Eggplant, 240
Elderberry, 123
Eloise Butler Wildflower Garden and Bird Sanctuary, 161
Eupatorium, 180

F

Fertilizer, 236, 239, 241
Finch, purple, 132
Flowering quince, 136
Flies, 191
Flycatcher, great crested, 19
Foliage, 138
Forsythia, 136
Fritillary, 193, 195
    great spangled, 195

G

Gardening
    fall, 144–147
    green, 149, 212–213
    winter, 130–133
Gardens
    botanic, 154–157, 170–171
    pick-your-own, 162–167
        Cutting Garden, 166
        Fields of Flowers, 166
        Hellerick's Family Farm, 166
        Melick's Town Farm, 166
        Parlee Farms, 166
        Ridgefield Farm and Orchard, 166–167
        Spring Ledge Farm, 167
        Take Your Pick Flower Farm, 167
        Wildseed Farms, 167
        Your Vase or Mine, 167
    vegetable, 224–247
Ginger, European, 143
Gladioli, 164
Goatsbeard, 142
Goldenrod, 124, 180
Goldfinch, 132
    American, 28, 30
Grapes, 243
Great Florida Birding Trail, The, 175
Great Texas Wildlife Trails, 175
Grass, 130–133, 192–193
    blue oat, 133
    feather reed, 133
    fountain, 133
    hakone, 143
    Japanese silver, 132, 133
    Mexican feather, 133
    ornamental, 52, 130–133
Grosbeak, 19

H

Hairstreak, 192, 197
    coral, 193
    striped, 193
Harrison, George
    berries for birds, 19
    birding advice, 38–39
    frugal tips, 55
    nesting habits, 12–15

Hawthorn, Washington, 19
Helianthus, 180
Hens-and-chicks, 52, 129
Herbs, 138, 227
Hibiscus, 104
Hollyhock, 53, 122, 193, 194
Honeysuckle, 124
    trumpet, 99
Host plants, butterfly, 122–123, 192–195
Hosta, 128
Hummingbird, 90–93, 108–114
    Allen's, 91
    Anna's, 92
    attracting, 53, 94–95, 96–107, 114, 143
    black-chinned, 92
    blue-throated, 115
    broad-tailed, 91, 115
    calliope, 92
    Costa's, 91
    facts about, 114
    food for, 55, 114
    hand-feeding, 94–95
    photography, 96–101
    ruby-throated, 27, 92, 96–101
    rufous, 93
Hyacinth, 137

I

Impatiens, 143
Indian Boundary Prairies, 161
Insects, 188–191
Iris, dwarf lake, 159

J

Jay, blue, 19
Joe Pye weed, 53, 194
Johnny-jump-up, 195
Junco, 132
Juniper, 129

K

Kale, 243
Kankakee Sands, 161
Katydid, broad-winged, 191
Killdeer, 14
Kingbird, 19

Kingfisher, belted, 12
Kitty Todd Nature Preserve, 161

L

Lacewing, green, 191
Lantana, 52, 183
Larkspur, giant, 66
Lavender, 123
Legume, 193
Lettuce, 139, 240, 243
Liatris, 53
Lilac, 136
Lily, 67
    asiatic, 165
    checkered, 137
    toad, 142
Loon, common, 28
Lungwort, 142

M

Malachite, 196
Mallows, 193
Manzanita, 19
Marigolds, French, 66
Milkweed, 124, 184–187, 194, 197
Missouri Botanical Garden, 156, 171
Mockingbird, northern, 19
Monarch, 180–181, 184–187, 192
    attracting, 180–181
    migration, 184–187
Morning glory, 67
Mosaic, steppingstone, 216–217
Mosquito, 189
Moss, 213
Moth, 123
    hawk, 122
    hummingbird, 123
    sphinx, 123
Mourning cloak, 192
Murre, common, 14
Mustard, 193
Myers, Melinda
    fall gardening, 144–147
    frugal tips, 55
    mixing veggies and blooms,
        138–139
    green garden trends, 149
Myrtle, southern wax, 19

N

Nanking Cherry, 137
Nectarines, 243
Nesting, 12–15, 132
    American coot, 14
    Atlantic puffin, 14
    bald eagle, 12–13
    Baltimore oriole, 14
    belted kingfisher, 12
    bluebird, 39
    brown-headed cowbird, 15
    burrowing owl, 12
    chimney swift, 14
    cliff swallow, 14
    common murre, 14
    great horned owl, 14
    killdeer, 14
    marsh wren, 15
    plover, 15
    whip-poor-will, 15
New Jersey tea, 193, 197
New York Botanical Garden, 157
New York ironweed, 180, 194
Nuthatch, white-breasted, 26

O

Olbrich Botanical Gardens, 157, 170
Onion, 232, 239, 240
Oregon Coast Birding Trail, 173–175
Organic, 243
Oriole, 19
    attracting, 8–10, 209
    Baltimore, 8–10, 14–15
        attracting, 125
    Bullock's, 8–11
    food for, 55, 57, 209
    hooded, 9–11
    orchard, 9–11
    Scott's, 9–11
Owl, 34–37
    burrowing, 12, 37
    great gray, 37
    great horned, 14, 36
    short-eared, 34–35
    snowy, 36–37

P

Painted lady, 122
Pansy, 138, 195
Pasque flower, 53
Pea, sugar snap, 139, 233
Peaches, 243
Pear, 197, 243
Penstemon, 53, 105, 124
Peony, 105, 165
Peppers, 139, 232, 240
    sweet bell, 243
Perennials, 63, 124, 140–143, 146–147,
    180, 194
    for attracting butterflies, 194
Pests, garden, 149
Petunia, 128
Phlox, garden, 104
Photography, 70–85, 172–175
    bird, 70–73, 172–175
    flower, 80–81
    how-to, 70–85, 96–101, 174
    hummingbird, 96–101
Plants
    dividing, 147
    drought-tolerant, 133
    easy-care, 126–129
    for attracting birds, 53, 56, 120–125,
        142
    for attracting butterflies, 120–125,
        129, 142–143, 180–181, 182–183,
        194
    for attracting hummingbirds, 99,
        102–107, 142–143
    for fall, 144–147
    for shade, 140–143
    for small spaces, 240
    for winter, 130–133
    late-blooming, 180–181
    low-cost, 50–53, 64–67
    photography, 80–81, 84–85
    spring-blooming, 134–137
Plover, 15
Polka dot plant, 143
Pollination, 241
Poppy, oriental, 104
Potato, 139, 243
    sweet, 243
Projects, 202–207
    bird feeder, 214–215
    birdbath, 220–221
    birdhouse, 212–213
    hummingbird feeder, 94–95

oriole feeder, 209
   steppingstone, 216-217
   suet feeder, 218-219
   wagon picnic table, 208
   wind chime, 210-211
Puffin, Atlantic, 14
Pumpkin, 139

Q

Quail, 132

R

Radish, 139
Raspberry, 197
Recycling, 44-49, 55, 56-62,
   149, 202-207, 210-211,
   214-215, 218-219
Redbud, 122, 125
Red-spotted purple, 193
Ridges Sanctuary, The, 159-160
Robin, American, 19, 26
Rodger's flower, 143
Rose, 67
   David Austin, 164
   moss, 66

S

Sage, 67
Salvia, 99
Sara orangetip, 196
Sedum, 52, 129
Seed starting, 58, 64-67, 129, 230-233
Seeds, 132, 205, 227, 240, 243
Serviceberry, 19
Shrubs, 122-123, 129, 134-137, 147,
   180, 192-193
   New Jersey tea, 193
Skipper, 123, 192-193
   checkered, 193
   duskywing, 192-193
   open-winged, 193
   powdered, 193
Solomon's seal, 142
Snapdragon, 67
Snowdrop, 137
Soil, 226, 241
Southeastern Arizona Birding Trail,
   175

Sparrow, 132
   white-crowned, 19
   white-throated, 19
Spice bush, 19
Spinach, 240, 243
Spirea, 129
   bridal wreath, 136
Spring azure, 122-123, 193
Squash, 239, 240
   butternut, 143
   summer, 233
Squirrels, deterring, 38, 55
Stokesia, 53
Strawberry, 243
Succulents, 56, 213
Suet, 55, 218-219
Sulphurs, 192-193
Sunflower, 56, 66, 139, 164
   Mexican, 56
Swallow
   cliff, 14
   tree, 19
Swallowtail, 123
   Canadian tiger, 193
   eastern tiger, 193
   western tiger, 192
   zebra, 196
Sweet pea, 165
Sweetbay, 19
Swift, chimney, 14
Switchgrass, 133

T

Tanager, 19
Thrasher, brown, 19
Titmouse, 19
   tufted, 32
Tomatoes, 239-241
   cherry, 139
   heirloom, 232
Tortoiseshell
   Compton's, 192
   Milbert's, 196
Towhee, 19, 132
Travel, 154-175
Trees, 122-123, 129, 147, 192
   fringe, 122
   oak, 192
   weeping willow, 192
   wild cherry, 193
Tulip, 137
Turtlehead, 180

U

University of British Columbia
   Botanical Garden, 157

V

Vegetables, 138-139, 146, 149,
   224-247
Verbena, 124, 183
Viburnum, 123
Viceroy, 192
Violets, 193, 195
Vireo, 19
Virginia creeper, 19, 124

W

Warbler
   myrtle, 19
   yellow-rumped, 19
Watering, 63, 237, 241
Waxwing, cedar, 19
Weigela, 137
Whip-poor-will, 15
Wildflowers, 158-167
Willow, 192
Winterberry, 19
Witchhazel, vernal, 136
Wishbone flower, 143
Wisteria, 193
Wood nymph, 193
Woodpecker
   downy, 19
   pileated, 19, 30
   red-bellied, 19
   red-headed, 24, 31
Wren, marsh, 15

Y

Yarrow, 53, 105, 124, 128, 164
Yerba Buena Gardens, 170
Yucca, 52, 128

Z

Zilker Botanical Garden, 171
Zinnia, 66, 124, 129, 164

There's something about birds

There's something about birds
That makes you want to sing
About what's in your heart,
Each happy little thing.
There's something about birds
That makes you want to fly
Over the whole earth,
Then up into the sky.
There's something about birds
That makes you want to be
Just like one—and fill
The world with poetry.

Poem by Marion Schoeberlein, Elmhurst, Illinois
Photo by Carol L. Edwards